CENTRAL ADMINISTRATION OF THE MUGHALS

A Brief Study

Dr. Samir Kumar Verma

All rights reserved. No part of this publication may be reproduced, stored in a retrieval system, or transmitted, in any form, or by any means, electronic, mechanical, photocopying, recording or otherwise, without the prior permission of the publishers.

ISBN: 978-93-95242-44-8
eISBN: 978-93-95242-46-2

©Author

Prabhakar Prakashan (P) Ltd.
Plot No.-55, Main Mother Dairy Road
Pandav Nagar, East Delhi-110092
Phone: 011-40395855, +4049916623
WhatsApp: +91 8368220032
E-mail: sales@pharosbooks.in
Website: www.prabhakarprakashan.com
First Edition: 2022

Printed By: Sushma Book Binding House, Okhla Industrial Area, Phase II, New Delhi-110020

Central Administration of the Mughals : A Brief Study
Dr. Samir Kumar Verma

PREFACE

This book has been written to discuss a number of controversial problems that existed in the Central Administration during the Mughal period in greater detail and I hope that a more satisfactory interpretation of the available data has been offered. Besides, an attempt has been made to create a synthesis in the data and to bring out the logical correlation among the different institutions.

To be candid, however, no effort has been made to include all the available details in the study. In view of the extensive nature of the accessible material, this would have been impossible. Besides, it would have marred the general effect and the book would have read like a dictionary of Mughal administrative jargon. However, the availability of these details will help the reader in understanding the nature of the institutions. Nevertheless, the attempt has been made to describe the mansion, not to count its bricks.

The book embodies four chapters dealing with the historical background, position of the Mughal emperor, different departments of the Central government, and nature of the central administration. Needless to say that the Mughal government was a highly centralized autocracy. The emperor was the pivot of the entire administrative machinery. The administrative system was in the nature of a military rule and was necessarily a centralized despotism.

This book will help the students who wish to go for their research work in this particular field of study and the teachers in their course plans in colleges.

I am thankful to all my Professors in the Department of History who taught me during my Research period and infused me with the knowledge of Medieval History that has helped me to write this book. My most sincere regards go to my wife Mrs. Nilu Verma for being so cooperative. It was only because of her inspiration and enthusiasm that this book could be completed.

Dr. Samir Kumar Verma

CONTENTS

CHAPTER-I

HISTORICAL BACKGROUND

The first three centuries of Turkish rule in India exhibit a similarity to the course of human life with its three stages of birth and adolescence, vigorous youth, and crabbed old age. During the first century, the Empire established by men like Muhammad Ghori and Qutubuddin Aibak was nourished and nurtured by men like Iltutmish and Balban (1200-1290). In its period of youth (1290-1380), it was consolidated and strengthened by rulers like Alauddin Khalji, Muhammad Tughlaq and Firoz. Then came old age. It had just set in when Timur's invasion (1398) struck it like palsy; thereafter for half a century, the Sultanate began to live as if on crutches. It showed some signs of recovery under the Lodis (1451-1525); but that was like the last flicker of the dying lamp. Babur's guns at Panipat sounded its death-knell.

The process of political disintegration had commenced during the reign of Firoz Tughlaq himself (1351-1388). He failed to reclaim the Deccan and frittered away his energies in fruitless campaigns in far-off regions of Orissa, Nagarkot and Thatta without being able to add a patch of territory to his shrunken empire. His revival of the Jagirs and enrolment of an army of slaves destroyed the merits of the reforms of the Khaljis and strengthened the forces of disorder. In his zeal for piety, he lightened punishment and thereby encouraged corruption in administration and inefficiency in the army.[1] To these unhappy circumstances was added an element of misfortune. During his last days, he lost his faculties of decision, and after his death a ten years' war of succession made confusion worse confounded.

First Tughlaq attained deliverance from the tortures of existence on Sunday, 20th September 1388[2] and was buried near the Hauz-i-Khas.[3] Because of the loss of faculties sometime before his death at the age of 81, Prince Muhammad had assumed regal authority with the title of Nasiruddin Muhammad Shah.[4] Sultan nominated his grandson, prince Tughlaq Shah, son of his elder son Fateh Khan, as his successor. On Firoz's death, Tughlaq Shah ascended the throne with the title of Sultan Ghiyasuddin. His uncle Nasir-ud-din Muhammad opposed his succession to the throne but he was defeated and he ran away to Kangra. It was under these circumstances that Abu Bakr Shah became king on 19th February 1389. A conspiracy was hatched against Abu Bakr and when he came to know of it, he retired with his followers to Mewat and it was under these circumstances that Nasir-ud-din Muhammad entered the capital and was enthroned in the palace of Firuzabad on 31st August 1390. He ruled for about four years from 1390 to 1394. His son ascended the throne at Delhi on 22nd January 1394 under the title of Ala-ud-Din Sikandar Shah. His reign was brief. He fell sick almost immediately after his accession and died on 8th March 1394. The vacant throne now fell to the lot of Prince Mahmud, the younger son of Nasir-ud-din Muhammad.

---

1. Shama Siraj Afif, *Tarikh-i-Firoz Shahi,* p. 303.
2. Yahya, *Tarikh-i-Mubarak Shahi,* p. 140.
3. Badaoni and Ferishta says that he was more than ninety at the time of his death. According to Afif he was born in 707 H (1307-8). At the time of his death he must have been in his 84tbh lunar and 81st solar year.
4. Yahya, *op. cit.,* pp. 138-40.

This was the state of affairs at Delhi when in October 1398 news was received that Timur had crossed the Indus, the Chenab and the Ravi and occupied Multan. He crossed the Jamuna on 15th December 1398 and the horrible sack of Delhi ensued. So complete was the destruction that the city was utterly ruined and those of the inhabitants who were left died, while for two whole months not a bird moved wings in Delhi.[5] After the departure of Timur, Nusrat Shah occupied Delhi but he was driven out by Mallu Iqbal. After the death of Mallu Iqbal in 1405, the affairs of Delhi were controlled by a body of nobles headed by Daulat Khan Lodi and Ikhtiyar Khan.

Khizr Khan (1414-1421) was not only the founder of the Sayyid dynasty but also its ablest ruler. Firishta says, "People were happy and contented under his rule and so the young and the old, the slave and the free condoled his death by wearing black garments.[6] Khizr Khan was succeeded by his son Mubarak Shah who proved to be the ablest king of the house of the Khizr Khan.

Bahlol Lodi was the founder of the Lodi dynasty which lasted from 1451 to 1526. According to the author of Tarikh-i-Daudi, "In his social meetings, he never sat on a throne and would not allow his nobles to stand; and even during the public audience he did not occupy the throne, but seated himself upon a carpet. Whenever he wrote a firman to his nobles, he addressed them as Mansad-e-Ala, and if at any time they were displeased with him, he tried so hard to pacify them that he would himself go to their houses, ungird his sword from his waist, and place it before the offended party; may, he would sometimes even take off his turban from his head and solicit forgiveness: 'If you think me unworthy of the station I occupy, choose one else, and bestow on me some other office'. He maintained brotherly intercourse with his chiefs and soldiers. If anyone was ill, he would himself go and attend

5. K.S. Lal, *Twilight of the Sultanate,* p. 21.
6. *Ibid.*

on him".[7] What is more to his credit, he was no mere militarist or warlord. He was a man of humane spirit and wanted to promote the public welfare by ensuring law and order, administering justice and refraining from burdening his people with insupportable taxes. To the poor and the indigent, he was always kind and generous. In short, he was a fairly popular and successful monarch.[8]

Bahlol Lodi was succeeded by his son Nizam Khan who took up the title of Sikandar Shah. He was able to find some time to look to the administration. He insisted on the auditing of the accounts of the Afghan nobles even at the risk of their displeasure. The author of Tarikh-i-Daudi tells us, "Every business had its appointed time and custom once fixed was never changed. When the Sultan had once allowed a particular meat or drink, he never altered it. A man of note came from Jaunpur to visit him in the hot weather and was given 6 jars of sherbet with his food on account of the heat and thirst; but when he came again in winter, he still had six jars of sherbet to drink. The Sultan always behaved to the nobles and great men in exactly the same way for many years as he did on the first day."[9] The Sultan daily received an account of the prices of all things and an account of what had happened in the different districts of the Empire. If he perceived the slightest appearance of anything wrong, he caused instant inquiries to be made about it. In his reign, business was carried on in a peaceful, honest, straightforward way. The study of belles-lettres was not neglected. Factory establishments were so encouraged that all the young nobles and soldiers were engaged in useful work. All the nobles and soldiers of Sikandar were satisfied. Professor K.A. Nizami says that Sikandar Lodi was in certain respects a very striking figure of medieval India. He gave a new orientation to Afghan policy in India and considerably raised the stature and dignity of the office of the Sultan. The Afghan nobility was made

7. *Ibid.*
8. A.B. Pandey, *The First Afghan Empire in India (1451-1526)*, pp. 27-28.
9. *Ibid.*

to recognize the superior status of the monarch. It was impressed upon the nobles that they were the servants of the Sultan and their position and power depended entirely on his goodwill and pleasure. Those who held Jagirs were required to submit accounts regularly and all cases of mismanagement, correction and misbehaviour were sternly dealt with. Sikandar Lodi was an able administrator. He could analyse the situation with a clear head and enforce his orders vigorously. He displayed a great sense of responsibility in discharging the functions of his office and for that, he worked very hard. The result was that there was peace and prosperity in the country. The common man got justice and the highways became safe from bandits and robbers. According to Sir Wolseley Haig, "He was the greatest of the three kings of his house and carried out with conspicuous success the task left unfinished by his father."[10]

After the death of Sikandar Shah, his eldest son, Ibrahim, was put on the throne on 21st November 1517 with the unanimous consent of the Afghan nobles and he took up the title of Ibrahim Shah. He wanted to strengthen his position at the cost of his nobles and he did all that he could to humble them. He was intelligent, courageous and brave. He had a reputation for piety and orthodoxy. He had a certain amount of vanity and he demanded more implicit obedience than was customary among the Afghans. He was reckless in punishing all those whom he suspected of the treachery of disaffection. In political dealings, he neither forgave nor forgot and hence he often appeared vindictive. His treatment of the nobility was on the whole tactless and indiscreet. He could make enemies but could not convert men of doubtful loyalty into devoted servants by his magnanimity. He attached too much importance to discipline, obedience and humility among his subordinates but did not know how to secure them. His policy was calculated to provoke opposition and rebellion. One of his nobles Daulat Khan Lodi revolted and asked Babur to conquer India. The

10. Wolseley Haig, Cambridge History of India, Vol. III, p. 246.

author of Tarikh-i-Khan-i-Jahan Lodi states that the invitation to Kabul was sent through Alam Khan. The latter marched to Delhi but he was defeated by Ibrahim who himself was defeated in the battle of Panipat in 1526.

Rushbrook Williams ascribes the defeat of Ibrahim Lodi to the artillery of Babur. To quote him, "If there was one single material factor which more than any other conduced to his ultimate triumph in Hindustan, it was his powerful artillery." However, A.B. Pandey points out that Babur himself does not emphasize the role of artillery so much as that of archery, coupled with Ibrahim's utter incompetence as a general so that he neither moved nor halted according to plan.[11]

On the eve of Babur's invasion, India was parcelled out among numerous mutually warring states. There was no paramount power in the country and a struggle for supremacy was going on. India was not in a position to present a united front to any enemy who might possess the audacity and ambition to carve out an Empire for himself. Babur proved himself equal to the task and was triumphant at the battle of Panipat. The victory of Panipat laid the foundation of the great Mughal empire which in grandeur, power and culture was the greatest in the Muslim world and could even claim equality with the Roman empire.[12]

The development of political and administrative institutions during the Muslim rule in India was undisturbed and continuous. The frequent changes in dynasties were mere ripples on the surface under which stream of life followed steadily. Even when the Sultanate was overwhelmed by centrifugal forces and broke into fragments, the administrative institutions were not changed, only the quality of administration was affected.

A study of the institutions of the Delhi Sultanate is a difficult

11. Pandey, *op. cit.*, p. 211.
12. R.P. Tripathi, Rise and Fall of the Mughal Empire, p. 35.

problem and complicated task. Unlike the Mughal institutions where one can get enough material in the shape of official records, diaries, firmans, and foreign accounts, the political institutions prior to the Mughals suffer from a paucity of material. No doubt the chroniclers of the period have recorded the events but from their writings, it is evident that in their enthusiasm for the glorification of their master, the Sultan, and in their zeal for the victories of Islam, they hardly even thought of political institutions and their working. Nevertheless, with patience and by adding bit by bit it is possible to draw the framework and fill there in portions of administrative institutions.

The earliest in point of time is Tajul Mausir of Hasan Nizami completed towards the end of Iltutmish's reign. It contains the chief military events of the years 588-620 and, although extremely florid and ornamental in style, is generally correct in the meagre facts it narrates. The author came to India soon after the conquest of Delhi and commenced his work early in the reign of Qutubuddin to whom he dedicated it. Next comes Tabaqat-i-Nasiri of Minhaj-us-Siraj completed in 1260. It is a general history of the world, but its value consists in its contemporary account of the Shamsbani conquest of India and the subsequent history of the new kingdom in which the author held high ecclesiastical and judicial office. Khazain-ul-Futuh also called Tarikh-i-Alai was written by Abul Hasan popularly known as Amir Khusrau, and a contemporary of Ziauddin Barani. The author died in 1325 having lived through the reigns of Balban, Jalaluddin Khalji, Alauddin Khalji, Ghiyasuddin Tughlaq and Muhammad Tughlaq. Amir Khusrau was a poet, but being connected with government offices, he has introduced in his poems a considerable amount of historical matter as well. Khazain-ul-Futuh deals with the military campaigns of Alauddin Khalji and gives valuable information about the military organisation, mode of warfare and weapons, etc. Quiranus Sadain, Miftahul-Futuh, Ashiqa, Nuh Sipihr, Tughlaqnama and Ijaz-i-Khusraui are some of the other works of Amir Khusrau, which throw some valuable light on the spirit and working of the government.

Tarikh-i-Firuzshahi of Ziauddin Barani was completed in 1359 and is dedicated to Sultan Firuz Shah Tughlaq. The book covers a fairly long period and much of his information has been taken by later writers of the sixteenth and seventeenth centuries. Tarikh-i-Firuzshahi is very valuable for the study of administrative institutions. But his language is a peculiar mixture of Persian and Hindustani and is often difficult to comprehend what the author is trying to convey. Fatawa-i-Jahandari is another work of Ziauddin Barani that reserves notice. It deals with the legal aspect of monarchy and government; rather it tries to set an ideal that a Muslim monarch should try to follow.

Ibn Batuta came to India during the reign of Muhammad bin Tughlaq and wrote his account after he had left India. His account of India where he stayed for eight years affords invaluable material, especially for the period of Tughlaq's reign. However, Ibn Batuta's work Kitabul Rihala suffers from a great defect in as much as the author had a peculiar weakness for bazaar gossips and spared no pains to incorporate them in his narration whenever and wherever possible. But with all its defects and shortcomings. Kitabul Rihala remains a valuable source, as he held an appointment under the Tughlaq Sultan, and had also access to many eye-witnesses from whom he had drawn information.

Masalikul Absar Fi Mamalikul Ansar is another book of considerable importance by Shahabuddin Abul Abbas Ahmad. His information is based mainly on the information supplied to him by Sheikh Mubarak and Khojandi, who had first-hand information about government affairs. The only shortcoming of the book is that its author never personally visited India and drew his information from those who had been to India.

Tarikh-i-Firuz Shahi is another book of great importance by Shams-i-Siraj Afif. He had first-hand knowledge of the reign of

Sultan Firuz Shah and his book deals exclusively with the reign of that monarch. Futuhat-i-Firuz Shahi, Sirat-i-Firuz Shahi and Figh-i-Firuz Shahi, are also important sources for the study of the administrative system and the spirit of the government. Of these, the first is believed to have been the personal composition of the monarch and throws considerable light on the working of the mind of the Sultan in the direction of the administration. The second work is believed to be the result of the Sultan's dictation and throws some light on the working of the government. The third one embodies the orthodox view and in a way depicts the theoretical aspect of the government.

Among the Insha literature of the period, mention must be made of Insha-i-Mahru which Afif mentions as Tarassul-i-Ainul-Mulki. It is a collection of letters compiled by Ainul-Mulk "Mahru' who was a military officer and an administrator and came into prominence in the reign of Alauddin Khalji and continued to serve the government till his last days during the reign of Firuz Shah Tughlag. It contains 133 letters of which 12 letters are written on behalf of Sultan Firuz Shah, one on behalf of Malikus Shark Shihabuddaula and the rest are by the author addressed to various officers and religious men. These letters contain useful information about economic, social and administrative matters. These letters inform us about the corrupt practices that had entered the administration during the reign of Firuz Shah.

Tarikh-i-Mubarak Shahi of Yahia-bin Ahmad bin Abdullah Sirhindi was compiled and dedicated to Sultan Mubarak Shah Sayyid in 1433, but subsequently, the author added some portions and brought it up to 1434. Similarly, Tarikh-i-Muhammadi of Muhammad Bihamad Khani informs us of the state of affairs up to 1439 and heeps us to ascertain the position of the government officers during the period after the Tughlaqs.

Of the later chronicles, mention must be made of Tabaqat-i-Akbari of Nizamuddin Ahmad, Muntakhabut Tawarikh of Abdul

Qadir Badauni and Gulshan-i-Ibrahimi or Tarikh-i-Firishta of Muhammad Qasim-bin-Hindu Shah alias Firishta. For the period of the Lodis, one has to depend on later works like Tarikh-i-Daudi of Abdullah and Makhzan-i-Afghani of Niamatullah.[13]

Sri Ram Sharma has given a fairly full description of the source material on this period in his A Bibliography of Mughal India. As a matter of fact, the material is embarrassingly rich and has not been fully utilized. Here it would not be out of place to comment briefly on the more important works. Of these Abul Fazl's Akbarnamah gives a detailed description of the events in Akbar's reign. It is an accurate and true record of events, even though personal references to the monarch are couched in hyperbolic terms. After Abul Fazl's death, the narrative was completed by Inayat-ullah. The Akbarnamah throws considerable light upon administrative measures, it is indispensable to a writer on the Mughal government.

The Tuzuk-i-Jahangiri, being Jahangir's memoirs, contains a record of the emperor's impressions and measures. His frankness and regard for the truth make the book one of the most interesting essays in autobiography. It has numerous references to the monarch's administrative measures. For Shah Jahan's reign, we have the Padshahnamah. Shah Jahan first entrusted the work to Mirza Amina Qazwini who covered the emperor's life as a prince and the first ten years of the reign. Then Abd-ul-Hamid Lahuri was summoned from Patna where he was living in retirement and entrusted with the work. He wrote about twenty years of the reign in detail in the Padshahnamah. Chandra Bhan Brahman's work Chahar Chaman throws interesting light on the working of the administration in the reign of Shah Jahan. He was posted in the office of the chief diwan of the empire and knew the great Sad-ullah Khan personally. He served under four diwans in several capacities. For some time he was in-charge of the department for drafting farmans and thus had direct access to the emperor.

13. U.N. Day, *The Government of the Sultanate*, pp. 14-17.

Munshi Muhammad Kazim describes in his Alamgirnamah the events of the first ten years of Alamgir I's reign. The emperor, in keeping with his character, did not like the idea of an officially sponsored history of the reign, hence he asked Muhammad Kazim to discontinue the work. Muhammad Saqi Mustaid Khan wrote his Maathir-i-Alamgiri after the death of the monarch in which he deals with the rest of the reign.

Now we turn to books on general history which, however, throw special light on certain reigns. The first of these, Khwajah Nizamuddin Ahmad's Tabagat-e-Akbari is reliable but it does not interest itself in religious social or administrative matters. On the other hand, Abd-ul-Qadir al-Badaunis Muntakhab-ut-tawarikh is rich in reference to Akbar's religious policy and administrative policy. He wrote his book with the set purpose of placing on record Akbar's aberrations from orthodox Islam. He has taken the main events from Khwajah Nizam-ud-din Ahmad which he has hung his disapproval of the monarch's errors. A work of considerable importance is Muhammad Hashim Khan's Muntakhab-ul-lubab which throws welcome light on Alamgir I's reign. Muhammad Hashim Khan is better known as Khawafi Khan. The book is a fair evaluation of the reign and is nowhere defamatory, malicious or too critical. It is not even disrespectful. Nimat Khan Ali's Waqai is a continuous satire. The Muntakhab-ul-lubab is rich in giving details of administrative measures and is of considerable value.

There is considerable source material on administration itself. The place of pride is held by Abul Fazl's Ain-I-Akbari which the author intended to form a supplement to his Akbarnamah. It is almost an encyclopaedia of Akbar's reign, covering philosophy, religion, geography, administrative institutions, agricultural and industrial products and a host of miscellaneous data. It is more than a gazetteer of the empire. The availability of official records and returns to the author makes the Ain one of the most reliable documents of history in any language. Another work of great interest is Mirat-i-Ahmadi by Mirza Muhammad Hasan alias Ali Muhammad Khan Bahadur. He was the diwan of Gujarat in the reign of Muhammad Shah and, therefore, was familiar with the working of the provincial government. It reproduces some farmans of Alamgir's reign which are of primary importance in understanding the nature of the agrarian administration.

There are other treatises on various aspects of the Mughal administration. Some of these are called dastur-ul-amals, or manuals of administration, others give statistical data, and yet others describe either certain institutions or the functions of some central, provincial, sarkar, parganah and village officials. There is hardly an aspect of administration that is not covered by this literature. The importance of this literature cannot be overemphasised. It would be cumbersome to describe all of these tracts and treatises, but a few important ones may be brought to notice. The Dawabit-i-Alamgiri (anonymous), Haqiqatha-i-Hindustan by Lachhmi Narayan Shafiq, Kaijiyat-i-Subajat-i-Mumalik-i-Mahrusah-i-Hindustan, Chhatar Mal's Diwan Pasand, Rajah Rup' (Who claims to be a disciple of the famous Todar Mal), Dastur-ul-Amal, another treatise by Khwajah Yasin and Najaf Ali's Risalah-i-Manasib have been found useful.

Of equal importance are the various collections of letters and documents. Of these most conspicuous are the letters of Alamgir I which throw a flood of light on the history of the period. Apart from the well-known Ruqqaat-i-Alamgiri of which there are several lithographed editions, there is Saiyid Najib Ashraf Nadwi's Ruqqaat-i-Alamgiri to which is appended a detailed introduction containing a good discussion of source materials as well as Prince Aurangzeb's character and relations with his father and brothers. Another collection is Muhammad Sadiq Ambalwi's Adab-i-Alamgiri. The compiler was secretary to Alamgir's son Prince Akbar. These letters were written for Aurangzeb by his secretary Qabil Khan. There are two collections by Inayat-ullah Khan, Ahkam-i-Alamgiri and Kalimat-i-Taqyibat. Ragaim-i-Karaim was compiled by Saiyid Ashraf Khan Mir Muhammad-al-Husaini. These letters were written to the compiler's father Mir Abd-ul-Karim The Dastur-ul-Amal-i-Agahi was compiled on the order of Raja Aya Mal, diwan of Rajah Siwai Jai Singh of Jaipur. This is by no means an exhaustive list of the collections of Alamgir's letters because there are several anonymous collections scattered in various libraries of the world.

Then there are a large number of documents like farmans, sanads and other certificates scattered in museums, libraries and private collections. Many families who were beneficiaries of grants of one kind or another have preserved such documents on their copies. A fair number have been preserved in inshas as models of elegant writing or of official correspondence. Of these a few deserve mention. Ruqqaat-i-Tahir Wahid was at one time known to every school boy. Ruqqaat-i-Munshi and Majma-ul-Afkar are preserved in Khuda Bakhsh Public Library, Patna. Izad Bakhsh Rasa's Riyad-ul-Widad is fairly common. Haft Anjuman by Talivar and Insha-i-Rushan Kalam by Bhopat Rai are collections by Hindu officials, there are also a few anonymous collections which contain much useful material. The state archives of Jaipur contain a large number of letters of Shah Jahan and Alamgir I as well as newsletters regarding important events.

A number of European travellers came to the empire whose writings have been published. Some of them have left voluminous descriptions of what they heard and saw. These accounts are of little use as source material for history.

In the presence of an embarrassingly large quantity of original recorded source material, it is not necessary to rummage through epigraphy for an occasional ray of light. The use of numismatics and epigraphy is not denied, but in view of ample records it has not been necessary to base any important conclusions upon there. R.B. Whitehead's work on Mughal numismatics will always remain a classic. Another significant contribution is by Hodivala

The Mughal period has attracted comparatively more attention than the Sultanate and there are a number of modern works available. Apart from general works like the Cambridge History of India (volume IV), there are monographs on each reign. There is Vincent Smith's Akbar, Beni Prasad's Jahangir, Banarsi Prasad Sakson's Shah Jahan and Faruki's Aurangzeb and His Times. Then there is Jadunath Sarkar's voluminous History of Aurangzeb. Vincent Smith's Akbar is a comprehensive work, but it suffers from serious drawbacks. It was written almost half a century ago and a good deal of research has taken place since then. His preference for European sources has led him quite often to conclusions which have been proved to be wrong. In the matter of administration, because he has relied heavily on translations, too many errors have crept into his statements. Beni Prasad's Jahangir also was written many years ago, but it is more sound and has stood the test of time better. Banarsi Prasad Saksena's Shah Jahan is comparatively more recent and it gives a readable account of the reign. Faruki has brought in new material but his book is amateurish and lacks confidence. It is apologetic which mars its value. Jadunath Sarkar's reputation was built on his book on Alamgir-I and it has considerable material.[14]

A good deal has also been written on the Mughal administration and some of its particular branches. Jadunath Sarkar was the first in the field so far as a monograph on the administration as a whole is concerned. It has a good deal of stray information mostly based on eighteenth-century materials, but the book's main fault is that it lacks synthesis and fails to give any insight into the logic of the administrative organization. It describes, as if it were, bricks rather than the building Ibn Hasan's The Central Structure of the Mughal Empire set a new standard in writings on the history of the Mughal administration and its study is profitable even now. S.A.Q. Husaini's Administration under the Mughals is well written and has the

14. I.H. Qureshi, *The Administration of the Mughal Empire,* pp. 19-21.

additional advantage of relating Mughal institutions to their Muslim origins. Sri Ram Sharma's Mughal Government and Administration is the latest book on the subject in the field.

There are certain works on some particular problems. Abdul Aziz has one study of the treasures etc. of the Mughals and another of the mansabdari system. Both of these are helpful and reliable. Irvine has a book on the Mughal army which is mostly based on the eighteenth century in detail. Irvine's understanding of the mansabdari system is defective. Moreland's The Agrarian System of Moslem India is an excellent book and has removed many cobwebs of misunderstanding. However, the book was written more than a quarter of a century ago and our understanding of the system has been gained through further research. Moreland's two other books India at the Death of Akbar and from Akbar to Aurangzeb are in a different category. Irfan Habib has collected a good deal of detailed information in his Agrarian System of Mughal India.

Abul Fazl was the author of Akbarnamah. He was born in 1551. He was introduced to Akbar in 1575 and he rose to a position of eminence. He distinguished himself as a writer, statesman, diplomat and military commander. He was assassinated in 1602.

Abul Fazl made thorough preparations for writing Akbarnamah. To quote him "Assuredly, I spent much labour and research in collecting the records and narrative of his Majesty's actions and I was a long time interrogating the servants of the state and the old members of the illustrious family. I examined both prudent, truth-speaking old men and active-minded, right-actioned young ones and reduced their statements to writing. The royal commands were issued to the provinces. I also took much trouble to incorporate many of the reports which ministers and high officials had submitted, about the affairs of the empire and the events of foreign countries..." Abul Fazl originally intended to write four volumes on the reign of Akbar. The fifth volume was to be devoted to administrative institutions established by Akbar. The original draft was revised five times before it was submitted to Akbar in 1596. Ain-i-Akbari was compiled earlier and submitted in 1593.

Akbarnamah is a detailed history of the reign of Akbar. The first part deals with the birth of Akbar and the reigns of Babur and Humayun. The second part deals with the reign of Akbar from the first to the end of the 46th year. The third part is the Ain-I-Akbari which, according to Garrett, will deservedly go down to posterity as a unique compilation of the system of administration and control throughout the various departments of government in a great empire faithfully and minutely recorded in their smallest detail, with such an array of facts illustrative of its extent, resources, conditions, population, industry and wealth as the abundant material supplied from official sources could furnish."[15]

The Akbarnamah is the most complete and authentic history of the reign of Akbar. The literary attainments of Abul Fazl, his acute and analytical mind, the position he had in the court and the confidence he enjoyed of his master, his great industry and honesty of purpose eminently fitted him to become the historiographer royal of the Mughals.

The Muntakhib-ut-Twarikh was written by Mulla Abdul Qadir of Badaun. The author was born in 1540. In 1574, he was introduced to Akbar who appointed him as Imam and gave him 1,000 bighas of land as Madad-i-Maash. Akbar was impressed by his learning and his ability to break the pride of learning of the Mullahs. However, he was thrown into the background by Abul Fazl. The result was that Abdul Qadir became the enemy of Akbar and he condemned Akbar, Abul Fazl and Faizi in the strongest possible language. He not only disliked the free thought and eclecticism of Akbar but was also disgusted with Akbar's patronage of men of different religions. He completed his work shortly before his death and according to Khafi Khan, its publication was suppressed by Jahangir.

---

15. Edwardes and Garrett, *Mughal Rule in India,* p. 45.

The Tabaqat-i-Akbari was written by Nizamuddin Bakshi in 1592-3. It is a general history beginning with the Ghaznavids and comes up to the end of the 36th year of the reign of Akbar. This work has been held in high repute for its sobriety and authentic account of the events of the period which it covers. It became the basis of future works. The author held important offices under Akbar and was held in high esteem.

Several factors contributed to the success of the Mughals in establishing their dynasty so firmly in India. The Sultanate had existed in stormy times. The Mongol inroads had unsettled the world of Islam. The Sultanate could not afford the luxury of dynastic stability because it needed strong men of action to meet the challenge. When, with the conversion of the Mongols to Islam and their adoption of civilized ways, the challenge seemed to weaken, it did not result in accession to the strength of any dynasty. It only produced disintegration. Provincial dynasties prospered, but Delhi itself fell prey to discord and conflict. In any case, the feeling that the danger had disappeared was only a delusion. Timur's invasion in 1398 demonstrated the fact that the zeal for the conquest had not exhausted itself in Central Asia. When the forces of law and order once again began to assert themselves and the Lodis began to succeed in extending their authority, they were thwarted by Babur's invasion in 1526. The lesson learnt by the Lodis was forgotten by the Surs, whose lack of cohesion and incapacity to unite gave Humayun his second opportunity in 1555.[16]

By the time Akbar established himself firmly, a balance of power emerged in the region. The Mughals, the Safawis and the Uzbegs were well established and each one of these was suspicious of the intentions of the other two. The Safawis had discovered, as the Mughals were to discover later, that a Central Asian adventure was not paying. The Uzbegs had been punished severely by the Safawis

16. I.H. Qureshi, *op. cit.*, pp. 2-5.

when Shaibani Khan and Shah Ismail had tried their strength. The Mughals had a wholesome respect for the Safawis as well because of their experience in Qandahar which they finally lost to Iran in 1653. The Mughals exercised considerable vigilance and were rewarded by the disinclination of their neighbours to undertake an invasion of their territories. The respite from external invasions was a source of great strength to the Mughals because all their resources could be diverted to the conquest of the subcontinent and consolidation of their power. This was made possible through the central administration of the Mughals.

CHAPTER-II

POSITION OF THE MUGHAL EMPEROR

The Indian concept of sovereignty and its evolution through the ages make an interesting study. The first reference to the origin of kingship is found in the Aitareya Brahmana, which clearly indicates election, by common consent, of the most suitable person to act as a ruler in an emergency.[17] In the Taittiriya Brahmana, there is an exposition of the divine origin of kingship.[18] Both these theories of the origin of kingship, viz., election and divine creation, are expounded in detail in the later political literature of India.[19] The Hindu king had to be virtuous and just, and had to act in accordance with the Dharma. "Strictly speaking", says Beni Prasad, "Hindu political theory vests sovereignty in the Dharma or law in the widest sense of the term. But administration was entrusted to the king.[20]

The Turks brought with them the Islamic theory of sovereignty, first to the Punjab under the Ghaznavids in the 11th century and then under the Ghorides at the end of the 12th and the beginning of the 13th centuries. The Arabs, who had conquered Sindh and Multan in 712-13, ruled as mere governors and were not confronted with the problem of reconciling their authority with the sovereignty of their liege-lord, the Caliph of Baghdad.

---

17. Aitareya Brahmana, vide H.C. of the Indian People, Vol. 1 (The Vedic Age), pp. 425-26.
18. Taittiriya Brahmana, *op. cit.,* p. 426.
19. Mahabharata, Shanti Parva, Section LIX, pp. 180-186.
20. Beni Prasad, *The Age of Imperial Unity,* p. 319.

Islam believes in a universal state. There can be, according to the strict Islamic theory, only one Muslim state in the world, and all Muslims are its citizens. It is designated as the 'dar-ul-Islam' or the realm of Islam, as opposed to the 'dar-ul-Harb' or the land of infidelity, and was subsequently called the Caliphate. God is its true, though invisible, king, and the actual earthly ruler, called the Khalifa (caliph), is merely his agent bound to administer the divine law as expressed in the Quran, which is, in Muslim eyes, the word of God revealed to their prophet, Muhammad. The divine law or Shar made up of Quranic injunctions and the sayings of Muhammad (hadis), is religious law; civil law, if any, is completely subordinated to it and merges its existence in the religious law. The Shar is eternal and immutable. The Caliph had no authority to change or even modify it. He could only interpret or amplify it. The Caliph was chosen by prominent Muslim leaders, and his election was confirmed by the general body of the faithful or millat in whom sovereignty was vested, and who could bestow in on any bona fide Muslim. Although there is no ordained clergy in Islam, there has always been a body of ulama or learned divines, who individually or collectively enjoy the right to issue a decree to the effect that the ruler has violated the Quranic law, and to ask the general body of Muslims to rebel against him. The jurists in Islamic polity are theologians, and masters of the Quran and the hadis (traditions). The ruler is the defender and maintainer of the faith, and its purity and integrity; he is the commander of the faithful (Muslims), the protector of the Caliphate, and its supreme judge. He is the chief executive of the realm. The Islamic State is thus a theocracy.[21]

---

21. I.H. Qureshi, Administration of the Sultanate of Delhi, pp. 42-44. Qureshi protests against the use of 'theocracy', and calls the Sultanate 'theocentric'. See A.L. Srivastava, Nature of the State in Medieval India, vide Uttara Bharati – a Journal of Research of the Universities of U.P., Vol. IV, No. 1, December 1957, pp. 1-7.

The Turkish rulers of Ghazni inherited through their Samanid over-lords of Khurasan, Turkistan and Trans-Oxiana, the Islamic theory of sovereignty and introduced in the Punjab the traditional Muslim institutions for its administration. Mahmud Ghazni, who assumed the title of Sultan, felt it necessary, in accordance with Islamic traditions, to secure the confirmation of his title from the Khalifa of Baghdad, and his successors followed his example. The Ghorides, who succeeded them, walked in their footsteps. Qutub-ud-din Aibak, who laid the foundation of the Sultanate of Delhi and assumed the royal dignity on 26 June 1206, received his insignia from Ghiyas-ud-din Mahmud, the nephew of his deceased master Muhammad of Ghur, and thus indirectly recognised the Khalifa of Baghdad as his suzerain. From the time of Iltutmish, the first Sultan of Delhi to receive the investiture as Sultan direct from the Khalifa in February 1229, almost every ruler of the Sultanate (1206-1526) except Qutub-ud-din Mubarak (1316-1320) acknowledged the overlordship of the Caliph, either of Baghdad or of Cairo. In 1258 the last Caliph of Baghdad, Mustasim, was put to death by the Mongol leader Hulagu Khan and yet the Indian Sultans continued to inscribe their names on their coins till 1296. Thereafter they recognised the new Abbasid Caliphate of Cairo (set up in 1261) until it was put to an end by the Sultan of Turkey who assumed the title of Khalifa in 1517.

The Sultan of Delhi from the time of Qutub-ud-din Aibak till the end of the Sultanate was in practice an independent sovereign, and the succession to the throne was not regulated by any external authority. The Caliph did in no case appoint a sultan, nor did he ever remove any. he was in fact powerless to do so. The principle of election for choosing the Sultan, which was found unworkable even in Damascus and Baghdad, broke down in India. Nomination and fitness faced a little better. There was, moreover, no fixed law of succession throughout the medieval period, and an element of uncertainty cropped up when a king died and the throne became vacant.

This theory of kingship being merely a human device, and the struggle and wars waged by the descendants of Iltutmish for attaining it for a quarter of a century could hardly have been conducive to producing in the people respect for the crown.[22] It was probably to remove this deficiency that Balban (1265-1287), who was a master of human psychology, placed kingship on an exalted plane. He claimed his descent from the mythical Khaqan Afrasiyab and the status of the viceregent of God (Zillillah).[23] To raise the prestige of the crown he modelled his court after the ancient Persian fashion and introduced the custom of pabos, i.e. of kissing the royal foot. The doctrine of super man, which was known to the Mongol Khaqans and was believed by the Hindus was for the first time adopted by this Sultan of Delhi. Whether this new element in the theory of kingship was retained after Balban one cannot definitely say, but it seems that it had come to stay, Qutub-ud-din Mubarak (1376-1320) assumed the title of Caliph and thus became the shadow of God (Zillillah) which was originally the prerogative of the Caliph. For some years Muhammad bin Tughlaq (1325-1351), following the example of Qutub-ud-din Mubarak, inscribed on his coins Al Sultan Zilli Allah[24] (Sultan the shadow of God), but abandoned the practice eventually. But courtiers and historians continued to ascribe high-sounding titles to almost all the sultans of Delhi from the time of Qutub-ud-din to the end of the Sultanate. It may be noted here that the belief originally held in the thirteenth century Hindustan that sovereignty was vested in the Albari branch of the Turkish race, was abandoned when power passed to the Khaljis. Competence and militarism became the basis of sovereignty from the time of the Khaljis to those of the Lodis and the Surs.

22. Courtiers and historians and Zillillah for Iltutmish and his successors, but the latter did not publicly assume the title.
23. Ziad-ud-din Barani, Fatawa-i-Jahandari, p. 70.
24. H. Nelson Wright, *Catalogue of the Indian Museum Coins,* Vol. III, pp. 58-59.

With the accession of the Lodis (1451), who were Afghans, there was a revolutionary change in the theory of kingship. The Afghan conception of kingship was that of a tribal monarchy and the king was chief among equal chiefs.[25] Bahlol Lodi would not sit on the throne in the presence of his nobles, and shared the royal carpet with them. He gave the monarchy the appearance of a tribal chiefship. Such a defective theory, which exalted the nobles to the status of semi-monarchs, did not work satisfactorily and fissiparous tendencies raised their heads among the nobles. Sikandar Lodi (1489-1517) had, therefore, made an attempt to restore the Turkish theory and in this, he attained some measure of success. But his son Ibrahim (1517-1526) offended his Afghan peers and lost his throne in the contest.

Babur inherited a theory of kingship that was a combination of the ideas of his ancestors—Timur the Turk and Changiz Khan the Mongol. The Mongols believed in the semi-divine origin of the family of Changiz Khan. The Great Khan, as the head of this house was called, ruled in Mongolia and was a political and military, not religious leader. Sovereignty was his birth right on account of the facts of centuries of history Timur's conception of sovereignty was influenced by Islamic traditions. He believed himself to be the viceregent of God and thought that since God is one and has no partner. His vice-regent on earth must be one.[26] He gloried in his title of the promoter and renovator (Murawwaj wa mujaddid) of the religion of Islam, and personally read the Khutba, in the manner of some of the Caliphs in his own name. Yet Timur kept the fiction of the over-lordship of the Great Mongol Khan alive, and did not adopt any higher titles than those of 'Amir' and 'Mirza': It was left to his grandson, Abu Saiyad Mirza, to assert that he was sovereign in his own right, and to disregard the ultimate, though nominal, sovereignty of the Mongol Yunus Khan. Babur, who inherited this concept of kingship from his paternal as well as maternal ancestors

25. A.L. Srivastava, *Akbar the Great,* Vol. II, p. 9.
26. Daudi, *Mulfusat-i-Timuri*, pp. 86-88.

and who was a believer in the hereditary right of sovereignty, went a step further, and in 1507 assumed formally the title of 'Padshah' (king).[27] It was practical politics to do so, as the Mongol Khan had been overshadowed by the dazzling success of the Uzbek leader Shaibani Khan and the rulers of the prominent neighbouring countries, like Persia, Trans-Oxiana and Turkey enjoyed the high sounding titles of 'Shah' 'Sultan' and 'Qaiser' respectively. But even before he assumed the title of 'Padsah' Babur, like his ancestors, had not recognised the legal superiority of the Caliph, dead or alive. He considered himself equal, if not superior, to the Sultan of Turkey who had adopted the title of Khalifa in 1517.

Humayun was less practical and more presumptuous than Babur. Although the Mughal dominion and authority had suffered diminution on account of the partition of the empire among his brothers, Humayun continued to believe, like his ancestors, that the king was the shadow of God on earth and that it was consequently his duty to do within his sphere as God did in relation to his creation. He even thought that being king he was the centre of the human world as the sun was that of the universe. He is said to have claimed divinity. At any rate, his court historian Khwandamir calls him 'His Majesty the shadow of God' and represents him as a personification of the spiritual and temporal sovereignty.[28] Humayun fancied that he received inspiration from God and that his institutions were the result of that inspiration. His son's court historian referred to him as 'the perfect man' (Insan-i-Kamil).[29] It is interesting to note that this Mughal King treated sovereignty as his personal property which he could bestow on anybody he pleased. He seated Nizam, the water carrier, who had saved his life at Chausa, on the throne for a few hours, with full powers to do what he pleased.

---

27. *Ibid.* See also *Babarnama*, Vol. I, p. 344.
28. Khwandamir, *Humayunnama,* Vol. I, p. 120.
29. *Ibid.,* p. 273.

Sher Shah (1540-1545) made no attempt to revive the Afghan theory of tribal leadership of the time of Bahlol Lodi. It was futile to put the hand of the clock back by half a century. Moreover, for about a generation the people had become accustomed to the Mughal theory of kingship according to which the king was no less than a shadow of God, and Sher Shah possessed practical good sense not to appear a mere tribal chief in the eyes of his nobles and people. At the same time, he was averse to alienating his Afghan comrades so he made a compromise, and assumed the title of Caliph of the age, i.e. the vice-regent of the prophet, not of God. He inscribed this title on his coins.[30] Islam Shah (1545-1554) followed in his father's footsteps and retained the title of Caliph. The power of the crown during the latter's reign increased so much that powerful nobles as well as high officials not only stood submissively before him at his court, but even showed respect to his slippers.[31] During the reigns of both these monarchs, the supremacy of Islam was maintained as an instrument of state policy.

Humayun's expulsion from his empire and his visit to the Safawid court established contacts between the Mughal court and Iran which led to a stream of Irani migrants to India in search of employment. The Mughal court, under the circumstances, could not remain a stronghold of orthodoxy, because the Irani immigrants were mostly Shiah. With the establishment of matrimonial alliances with the Rajputs and the growth of their influence at the court, the decline of the power of the orthodox Sadr-us-sudur was but a question of time. The position of orthodoxy had been challenged in the country by several movements of great proportions. Mohdawism had not been a weak adversary and the growth of the Bhakti Movement had softened the Muslim antipathy for the beliefs of the Hindus.[32] By its acceptance of the Sufic approach to

30. Wright, *op. cit.*, p. 109.
31. Abdul Qadir Badayuni, *Muntakhab-ut-Tawarikh,* Vol. I, p. 358.
32. For Mahdawisn, Erskine, ii, pp. 476-82. Tara Chand gives an excellent account of the Bhakti Movement. For a fuller discussion of heterodoxy under Akbar, see I.H. Qureshi, the Muslim Community of the Indo-Pakistan Subcontinent, chapter VI.

religion and turning it in favour of its own doctrine of all religions being the same in essence, it had created laxity and indifference among the Muslim masses, whose enthusiastic support could be the mainstay of the influence of orthodoxy at the court.

Naturally, all the opponents of orthodoxy combined themselves in their efforts to dethrone it. Shaikh Mubarak's family had suffered at the hands of the orthodox ulama at the court, and he and his sons Abul Fazl and Faizi worked skillfully to avenge themselves.[33] They found many allies in this effort; the historian Badauni who was such a critic of Akbar's heterodoxy was himself deeply tinged with Mahdawism and was no friend of the orthodox ulama at the court.[34] Indeed he was looked upon at the beginning as a likely instrument for overthrowing them. He did not prove useful because, like so many heresies in Islam, Mahdawism was itself exceedingly puritanical and fundamentalist in its beliefs and outlook. However, Abul Fazl found many allies among the non-Muslim and the non-Sunni Muslim courtiers and turned Akbar into an antagonist of orthodoxy.[35] Those who accuse Akbar of abjuring Islam go too far, their conclusions are not based upon sound evidence and they overlook many important facts which point in a different direction.[36] However, there can be little doubt about Akbar's feelings towards Makhdum-ul-mulk and Abd-un-Nabi and the School of thought represented by them. Even when allowance is made for Abul Fazl's animosity and Badauni's prejudice, the two theologians do not seem to be worthy representatives of the orthodox ulama nor qualified by their learning to hold their own against the brilliant attacks of more learned adversaries.[37] It

33. Blochmann,Biography of Abul Fazl in his translation of the Ain-i-Akbari.
34. *Ibid.*, p. ix.
35. Badauni is full of references to their leaders.
36. Badauni's descriptions of the debates in the Ibadatkhana (Hall of Worship) leave this impression, it would take too much space to give a description of their inability to defend orthodox doctrines. Later Shaikh Ahmed of Sirhind demonstrated how orthodoxy could be defended.
37. Kabir, Kamal and Dadu are only a few of numerous spiritual guide swho attracted men of diverse religions.

would, however, be misleading to attach too much importance to personal factors. Akbar was not the sole claimant of being a religious preceptor who could guide people to spiritual awakening irrespective of their religious affiliations, nor was he the greatest of those who had a following among diverse religious groups, but his position as a monarch and the atmosphere in his court produced political and administrative changes of considerable importance.[38]

The ostensible legal break from the past was a document drawn up by Shaikh Mubarak which was based upon a universally accepted principle.[39] In case the learned jurists differed and offered varying interpretations of the sacred text, the just monarch, technically described as imam-i-adil could choose any one of the interpretations offered. It is obvious that if there is no agreement or ijma on a point, and if the monarch's bonafide cannot be questioned and if he is capable of judging the merit of one interpretation against another, he must choose before he can enforce or apply a particular interpretation. There was nothing revolutionary in this principle, because it had always been accepted.

The document (The Infallibility Decree) was signed by several theologians, by some against their will, and was in the form of a statement by those assembled and present, hence it was called a mahjar. It was not because of the principle which was enunciated that the mahjar encountered opposition; it was considered a dishonest document because Akbar was mentioned as imam-i-adil, the just leader or ruler, who was invested with the authority to choose between several interpretations. According to Muslim jurisprudence, a monarch to be technically 'adil' for this purpose should have sufficient knowledge of the law to be able to judge the merits of the different interpretations. Akbar had no such qualifications. Besides, Shaikh Mubarak's intention was to undermine orthodoxy. Akbar had shown too great a predilection in favour of heterodoxy to leave any doubt about his

38. *Ibid.*

39. For the text vide Badauni, II, pp. 270-2.

choice. Monarchs who were not learned jurists had delegated the authority mentioned in the mandar to their Sadrs. With the signing of this mahjar, the orthodox ulema of the court sealed their fate. However, such a document was made possible by the decline in the influence of orthodoxy in the court and the realm. The Decree of Infallibility did vest the monarch with considerable power if his intentions were to uproot orthodox influence from the court. The mahjar limited the monarch's authority within the basic limits of the Muslim Law, the Quran and the agreed interpretations. The investment of an orthodox monarch with these powers would not have aroused such opposition. The document, however, remained a dead letter. It was never utilised. Akbar preferred to use the device of appointing men of pliable conscience as sadrs and judges to carry out his behests.

In his early days Akbar had, like his predecessors, considered it to be his duty as enjoined by the Shar not only to propagate Islam and to convert his non-Muslim subjects to that religion, but also to persecute those Muslims who had strayed from the orthodox Sunnism. We have it on the testimony of Akbar himself that during the first few years of his reign he had indulged in the policy of converting unwilling non-Muslims to Islam. He made a confession of this in his mature years and said: "Formerly I persecuted men into conformity with my faith and deemed it Islam. As I grew in knowledge, I was overwhelmed with shame. Not being a Muslim myself, it was unmeet to force others to become such. What constancy is to be expected from proselytes on compulsion?[40] That there was a good deal of persecution of Muslim heretics at Akbar's court is attested both by Abul Fazl and Badayuni. The Shia-Sunni conflict during Bairam Khan's regency and for sometime after Akbar had assumed the reins of government in his own hands, continued to man the atmosphere at the Mughal Court. In short, Akbar's legacy, ideological and administrative was a serious liability. It was a tremendous job to shake off the effects of an embarrassing legacy.

40. Abul Fazl, Ain-in-Akbari, Vol. III (2nd ed.), p. 429.

Akbar's theory of sovereignty was not the result of speculation. It was not borrowed ready-made from books; nor was it taken from any theorist or an adviser. It was born out of hard facts of life, and was the result of his own thought and innate practical common sense. He had seen with concern the refractory and rebellious conduct of his hereditary Muslim nobles and officials. From Shah Abul Maali to Ali Quli Khan Uzbek entitled Khan-i-Zaman, it was a long tale of insubordination and rebellion Akbar must have felt that he could not command the unswerving loyalty of his Mongol, Uzbek and Turkish nobility, and as for the Afghans, they were the sworn enemies of the Mughals. On the other hand, the Rajputs into whose intimate contact he had come after his marriage with an Amber princess early in February 1562, had given proof of their staunch loyalty. Akbar had witnessed the strange spectacle of Rajputs against their own kith and kin at the siege of Merta in February-March 1562. These hard facts impelled the young emperor to make a departure from the traditional Muslim policy towards the Hindus in practice, though not yet in theory. The consequent result was an edict sometime about the middle of 1562 forbidding the enslavement of prisoners of war and their conversion to Islam. This was followed by another important decree which abolished the pilgrims' tax on the Hindus in 1563. In March 1564. Akbar took the revolutionary step of abolishing the jizya, which knocked the bottom out of the foundation of the Islamic theory of discrimination against non-Muslims. Nevertheless, he did not as yet announce a formal change in the Islamic theory of kingship or even in that of the traditional system of administration. But a divergence between theory and practice could not continue for an indefinite period. Fortunately for Akbar, proof after proof was furnished of the staunch Hindu, especially Rajput, devotion in the shape of Rajputs fighting against Rajputs at Chittor (1567-68), at Ranthambhor and Kalinjar (1569) and at Haldi Ghati (1576) in furtherance of the interests of the

Mughal empire. On the contrary, rebellion after rebellion of his Muslim nobles and officials occurred almost continuously during the period. Akbar's brother-in-law Mirza Sharf-ud-din revolted in 1562 and joined hands with Shah Abul Maali, his maternal uncle Khwaja Muazzam displayed contumacy and defiance in 1564, Abdullah Khan Uzbek, governor of Malwa, rebelled in 1564, and other Uzbeks followed his example in 1565. Mirza Hakim invaded the Panjab the same year and a prolonged rebellion of the Mirzas for years disturbed the peace of the country. In view of these hard realities Akbar swung both in theory and practice in the direction of religious toleration, and in 1567 Abul Fazl save an indication of a change for the first time in his master's theory of kingship.

The enunciation of Akbar's theory of kingship made by Abul Fazl on behalf of his sovereign for the first time in 1567, was revolutionary in character in as much as it repealed the Islamic theory of sovereignty by laying down that one of the essentials of kingship was "to inaugurate universal peace (religious toleration, sulah-e-kul)" and "to regard all classes of men and all sects of religion with the single eye of favour and not be mother to some and be step-mother to others." It also deprecated the theory of race, birth and blood of Balban and other Albari Turks, and that of hereditary birth-right believed in by Changiz Khan, Timur and Babur. These factors were no doubt important, but not essential. Some other essentials of sovereignty, according to Akbar, were magnanimity, lofty benevolence, ability, character, rectitude, justice, etc., (which Akbar's brother Mirza Hakim did not possess), besides its being a gift from God. In the words of Abul Fazl, "Kingship is a gift of God and is not bestowed till many thousand grand requisites have been gathered together in an individual. Race and wealth and the assembling of a mob are not enough for this great position. It is clear to the wise that a few among the holy qualities are magnanimity, lofty benevolence, wide capacity, abundant tolerance, exalted understanding, innate graciousness, natural courage, justice, rectitude, strenuous labour, proper conduct, profound thoughtfulness, laudable overlooking (of offences) and acceptance of excuses. And with all those notes of perfection, of which a few out of many are mentioned in detail in the ancient books of ripe philosophers, so long as the subject of such encomiums has not wisdom sufficient to overpower improper desires and unbecoming anger he cannot be fit for this lofty office. And on coming to the exalted dignity if he does not inaugurate universal peace and if he does not regard all classes of men, and all sects of religion, with the single eye of favour and not be a mother to some and be step-mother to others he will not become fit for the exalted dignity. Thanks be to God. The holy personality of the Shahinshah is a fount of perfect qualities and a mine of holy principles. Volumes would not be sufficient to describe the glories of the Lord of the universe. How can an incidental reference be sufficient?"[41]

Like some of the prominent ancient Kshatriya families and their modern Rajput descendants who traced their origin to the sun and the moon, Akbar claimed to have descended from the sun through his celebrated female progenitor, Alanquwa. Therefore, his theory of divine origin was akin to that of many of his contemporary Rajput chiefs, such as the Sisodias of Mewar, the Rathors of Marwar and the Kachhwahas of Amber. His belief in his being the shadow of God, had, therefore, greater significance than that of Balban, Sher Shah and other former Muslim rulers of India.

Moreover, like the ancient kings of Persia Akbar believed that the fortune of kings was linked with the sun, the illuminator of the world. "A special grace", he said, "proceeds from the sun in favour of kings, and for this reason, they pray and consider it a worship of the Almighty, but the short-sighted are thereby scandalized."[42] And that was why Akbar revered the sun and the light. He said, "To light a candle is to commemorate the rising of the sun. To whomsoever the sun sets, what other remedy hath he but this."[43]

41. *Ibid.,* p. 285.
42. *Ibid.,* p. 435.
43. *Ibid.,* p. 443.

It will be clear from the above that Akbar's belief in the theory of his divine origin was substantial. Abul Fazl's enunciation that 'royalty is a light emanating from God and a ray from the sun, the illuminator of the universe.[44] It reveals clearly the dual meaning of Akbar's theory of the divine origin of kingship.

In summing up in a systematic manner his ideas of Akbar's theory of kingship. Abul Fazl writes, "No dignity is higher in the eyes of God than royalty and that kingship is essential for putting an end to human selfishness, strife, and unbecoming ambition. If royalty did not exist the storm of strife would never subside, nor selfish ambition disappear. Mankind being under the burden of lawlessness and lust, would sink into the pit of destruction; the world, this great market place, would lose its prosperity, and the whole earth become a barren waste."[45] This is the justification of monarchy Abu-I-Fazl then proceeds to distinguish a true king from a selfish one. Both have an army, a large treasure and various other appliances of government. In the realm of a true king, these things are lasting, but in that of the selfish one, they are transient. A true king does not have an attachment to these worldly things and considers it to be his duty to remove oppression and provide security and good government to the people, whereas, a selfish ruler considers wealth and power as the end and neglects his duty to his subjects.

Although Akbar had completely identified himself with India and her people, et like his ancestors Changiz Khan and Timur, he conceived the idea of a world empire. He was ambitious of acquiring the whole of the Deccan and thereafter conquering Central Asia, Turkey and Arabia. His plan was to proceed to Khurasan and Iraq and from there to lead an expedition to Samarqand and Khotan. Next, he wanted to measure swords with the Sultan of Turkey, whom he looked upon as his great rival. He did not tolerate the

44. *Ibid.*
45. *Ibid.*, p. 2.

reading of the Khutba in the name of the Sultan of Turkey at Mecca and Medina. That was why in his scheme of conquest he gave Arabia an important place. With this object in view he proposed an alliance between himself and the king of Portugal against the sultan of Turkey. He was also keen to establish friendly relations with the Pope and with the king of Spain. The policy of one world and one sovereign, as opposed to the multiplicity of states, was conceived by Akbar as early as 1574.

The scheme of the conquest of Central Asia, Arabia and Turkey remained a paper scheme. Nevertheless, it is a tribute to Akbar's political idealism that he could conceive the idea of a world government in the 16th century.

It must be said that Akbar's theory of kingship was one of benevolent, and to a great extent even enlightened despotism. He believed with the Prussian king Frederick the Great of the 18th century Germany that he was the first servant of the people, and that it was his duty to think and work hard for their welfare. It was his firm conviction that, in discharging his duty to the people, he was performing an act of divine worship. The theory was acclaimed by the people (except for a small group of Sunni fanatics), and its practical application gave India peace and unity, progress and prosperity.

In ancient India, great prestige was attached to the position of the monarch, and he enjoyed special honours and privileges. In view of the popular belief in his divine origin, the king's person was almost sacrosanct. The kingly office was looked upon as a sacred trust, and the monarch's entire time was supposed to be devoted to the welfare of the people. It was also laid down that the king should be accessible to the people, and not depend absolutely on his immediate officers in the matter of people's grievances and their welfare. The concentration of powers in his hands did not necessarily make a king an irresponsible tyrant. His powers were restricted by the law or the Dharma,[46] and by the sabha and the samiti. He had also to respect public opinion.

---

46. Manu, VII, pp. 14-24.

The Sultan of Delhi was a Muslim monarch and as such he had to follow the Quranic law not only in his personal life but also in the administration of the state. He had a concentration of wide powers in his hands. Despite his wide powers, the sultan had some limitations in the exercise of his authority. In the first place, he could not interfere with the personal law of his subjects. Secondly, it was his duty to follow the Quranic law, and if he strayed from it his Muslim subjects had the right to rebel against him and even to depose him. Thirdly, the ulema and the nobility exercised some check on his authority. Nevertheless the sultan was a through-going despot, and as long as he followed the Quranic law and was the master of a strong army, he was all powerful.

The Mughal rulers assumed the higher title of 'emperor' as against 'sultan' which was the title of the early Muslim rulers, and this raised the former high in the eyes of the people. Akbar's title was 'Shahanshah' and he was looked upon as something more than a mere mortal. Every morning people collected to have a look at his face (darshan) before starting their daily work. Vassals and feudatories, who were masters of large territories, paid him homage by either kissing his foot or touching it with their forehead. The highest Hindu rajas were designated by the Mughals as mere 'zamindars' in their official records and court chronicles. Hardly was anyone, barring the crown prince and sometimes the prime minister, allowed to sit in a formal darbar (court). All had to stand, each in his proper place, in the public audience hall (diwan-i-am). There was a halo of majesty around the emperor's person.

During the early years of his reign, Akbar followed the traditional duties of a Muslim monarch in conformity with the injunctions of Islamic law. But as he developed into an impartial ruler of all his people, he gradually gave up such duties as were the peculiar obligations of a Muslim monarch. For example, he no longer considered it desirable to propagate the teachings of Muhammad. He gave up such duties of upholding the supremacy and prestige of Islam and of converting 'dar-ul-Harb' into 'dar-ul-Islam'. His policy of conquest was now inspired by political and economic reasons, and not by religious considerations. He now emphasised two of his duties as most essential. These were the protection of all his people, irrespective of race, caste and creed, and the establishment of complete religious toleration for all and granting of equality of status to all religions in his empire. Akbar stressed his duty of equal protection of all his subjects and said that "all this autocracy and world-rule, this sword-bearing and clime-conquering are for the purpose of shepherding and for doing the work of watch and ward…"[47] Akbar considered himself the father of his people, and looked upon service to them as an act of divine worship. He set before himself the ideal of advancing the people's social, cultural and spiritual welfare as well as their material well-being. He posed tremendous powers and authority to carry out this obligation. For, he was the Commander-in-Chief of the royal armies, the executive and judicial head of the administration, and the chief interpreter of the Muslim law.

The Islamic ideas of monarchy were revived after Akbar's death. Even the mahjar vesting Akbar with the authority to choose between different interpretations of the shar was a compromise with Islamic legalism, because it was clothed in its language and based upon its principles. Akbar doid not invoke it; Jahangir never mentioned it; Shah Jahan's motives in respect of orthodoxy could not be questioned; Alamgir I was a learned jurist himself. These monarchs looked upon themselves as Muslim emperors and did not come into conflict with the Shar.[48] Jahangir has generally been painted by modern historians as almost completely devoid of Islamic feelings and indifferent to religion.

The Mughal emperors assumed the title of padshah. Abul Fazl explains the etymology by saying that pad signifies stability and possessions and shah means origin and lord; thus padshah is a lord or a king who is so powerful that he cannot be ousted by anyone. It was, however, used for a superior king, an emperor.[49]

47. Srivastava, *op. cit.*, p. 27.
48. Dodwell, *Cambridge History of India,* Vol. IV, pp. 230-1.
49. Blochmann, *op. cit.*, p. II.

How Akbar spent his time in the work of administration can be seen in his daily routine. Sometime after he had taken the reins of government in his hands, he fixed time for his manifold duties in order to be able to function in a systematic and efficient manner. But it was not until 1578 that he announced a daily routine of his activities, which was hardly disturbed, whether he was at court or engaged in a military campaign. Akbar's first act after rising from bed, about two hours before dawn, was to go through his private meditation and prayer, which were followed by ablutions and toilet that commenced about an hour and a half before sunrise. At sunrise he would have a short prayer and appear at the Balcony of salute (Jharokha-i-darshan) facing the sun in the east, where the people assembled down below to get a glimpse of him. Here he spent considerable time, usually for four hours and a half, transacting business, listening to the peoples' grievances and deciding cases that were brought before him, on the spot. From the Balcony of Salute he would go to the public audience hall (diwan-i-am) and hold a public darbar which would usually last for about one and a half hours.[50] Here he transacted official business, passed orders for appointment and promotion of officers, etc. He would then go to the harem where officers and servants of the female section of the royal household would call on him. The ladies also submitted their applications and Akbar passed orders on them. After this, he would retire for midday prayer, lunch and rest.[51]

In the afternoon the emperor inspected elephants, horses, camels, mules and other animals. These were paraded before him and he took note of their condition and asked questions about them. Thereafter he held a private darbar in the private audience hall (diwan-i-Khas) where two state business, but one of a

---

50. Abul Fazl says that the public darbar was sometimes held in the afternoon and sometimes in the night. But it is clear from the practice during the reigns of Jahangir and Shah Jahan that usually it was held immediately after jharokha-i-darshan.

51. *Akbarnamah,* Vol. III, p. 257.

confidential nature, was transacted. This was followed by sunset prayer and probably a brief interval of rest. He spent the first part of the night in the private chamber (Khilwat-Khana-l-Khas), where scholars, scientists, philosophers and deeply religious men held discussions, and Akbar asked questions on various topics.[52]

When the work of assembly was over, Akbar listened to music for some time. After his mid-night prayer, he retired to his private apartments for sleep and rest. His sleep did not last for more than three hours, and was, more like waking.

As the work of administration increased tremendously, Akbar in 1597 split up his duties, and parts of them were fixed for each day of the week. For example, he inspected horses on Sundays, and camels, mules and bullocks on Mondays. On Tuesdays he held a review of his troops, on Wednesdays he attended to the affairs of the revenue and finance department and on Thursdays he held the court of law and decided cases. On Fridays he granted interviews to the pious and needy people, and on Saturdays he inspected elephants and their stables. The rest of the routine was followed as fixed previously.[53] The commencement and the close of each duty of the royal programme were announced daily to the people by music (beating of drum) from the imperial music gallery.

It is clear that Akbar spent more than ten hours daily in the business of the state. In addition to this, he would keep on pondering in the midst of his recreations, how best to improve his administration and better the lot of the people. It is noteworthy that Akbar's routine became a model for his successors to follow. Jahangir and Shah Jahan looked up to him for inspiration and followed him with pride. Jahangir, until his declining health prevented him from attending to strenuous duties, was conscientious in the transaction of public business and, contrary to popular notions, was interested in religious discussions as well as devotional exercises. The impression created by certain writers that he was

52. *Ain-i-Akbari*, Vol. I (2nd ed.), p. 16.
53. *Akbarnamah*, Vol. III, p. 717.

a besotted drunkard is not true.[54] Even when he was unwell, he did not abstain from attending the jharokha-i-darshan, the diwan-i-am or the diwan-i-khas.[55] When the emperors did find themselves unequal to such an arduous life, the empire lost its vitality, because among the medley of causes, the character and calibre of the later emperors played an important role in the decline of the empire.

In order to be able to appreciate Akbar's administration and its effect on the fortune of the king, the country and the people, it is desirable to form a correct picture of some of the important royal institutions at work. Of these, the jharokha-i-darshan naturally takes the first place. It was a revival of an ancient Hindu custom the object of which was to enable the common people to have direct access to the king and to place their individual grievances or complaints before him without any hindrance or interference from the officers and the macebearers. Akbar consequently revived the custom of appearing before the public at sunrise. Abul Fazl writes that after his morning devolution the emperor showed himself "to people of all ranks". Quite a large number of men and women, soldiers, merchants, peasants, trades people and other professions gathered around the place patiently waiting to catch a glimpse of "His Majesty".[56] As he appeared they saluted humbly; some of them greeted him by prostration and others with the cry of 'Padshah' Salamat (long live the emperor). Badayuni records that many Brahmans, who looked upon Akbar as an incarnation of Rama or Krishna, would not have their breakfast without first catching a glimpse of him.[57] Many people thought it auspicious to begin the day's work by seeing the emperor's face first thing in the morning.

The institution of jharoka-i-darshan was like an informal darbar where Akbar transacted a good deal of official business. Two waqaya navises (writers) and some other officers had to be

54. Jahangir, p. 9, Mutamad Khan, p. 129.
55. Jahangir, p. 130.
56. *Ain Akbari,* Vol. I (2nd ed.), p. 164.
57. *Ibid.*

present on duty every day. Their main business was to take down not only the emperor's orders passed on various cases but also to record every word that fell from his lips. Akbar personally listened to complaints from individuals of both sexes and did them justice. From here the emperor would sometimes enjoy elephant combats and diverse other sports.[58] He utilised this institution for administering to the religious and medical needs of the people. All kinds of people would make offerings to the emperor in fulfilment of vows made to him and Akbar would gladly accept their little presents.[59] Thus the institution of jharokha-i-darshan serves a very useful political purpose by bringing the common people into personal touch with the ruler. It became a powerful cause of Akbar's enduring popularity. Akbar's successors, including the puritanical Aurangzeb, realized its importance and regained it.[60]

From the jharokha-i-darshan Akbar went to the diwan-i-am to hold a formal court which usually took about one and a half hours of his time. Although it was called public darbar everyone was not allowed to attend the court. Nobles, officials, sons, grandsons, and the grandees, who had the privilege of attending the darbar, saluted him by placing the palms of their right hands on their foreheads and standing in a respectful posture with their arms folded across their breasts. This method of salutation was called Kornish. There was a prescribed rule of etiquette, and absolute silence and discipline were observed. The work of the darbar started, according to an agenda prepared beforehand by the officer in charge. The officers of the various departments laid the papers of their proposals and read out their reports. Ambassadors from foreign countries were introduced and presented their credentials to the emperor. Dispatches received from the provinces and the fields of battle were read out. It is interesting to note that Akbar kept near the throne in the open darbar heaps of gold and silver coins to reward those whom he considered

58. *Ibid.*

59. *Ain-i-Akbari*, Vol. I (2nd ed.), p. 173.

60. Aurangzeb abandoned it a few years after his accession.

deserving.[61] A register containing the names and particulars of those who were given permission to attend the court was kept. Four or five secretaries or waqya navises noted down the proceedings of the court, and committed to writing the king's orders and in fact every word that he uttered.[62]

Diwan-i-Khas was a special court to which only ministers and nobles and sometimes very high officials, were invited. Occasionally, the royal princes also attended it. It was usually held in the afternoon, but sometimes it was convened in the evening. Here important administrative business of a confidential nature relating to revenue, finance and the army, and problems relating to foreign affairs, war and peace, were decided upon. The matters that were brought to the royal notice at the diwan-i-am were finally thrashed out and imperial farmans about them were drafted and received the royal assent and seal. Sometimes foreign ambassadors were received at this darbar, and the vassals of the highest category were also presented.

Another important royal institution was anjuman-i-dad-o-dihish or the assembly of expenditure which was held on certain special days. All sorts of people ranging from men of religion to worldly men, who attended this assembly, made requests to the emperor who presided over it. These requests were individually scrutinized and attended to.[63] Akbar did not believe in scattering gold indiscriminately. He gave monetary assistance to deserving people after ascertaining their conditions.

Attached to the household department were nearly 100 royal workshops, each of which was meant for manufacturing a special commodity needed for the army, the count and the imperial household. These workshops were situated near the palace. Some of them were exclusively for the manufacturing of arms and ammunition. Others were studies such as painting, calligraphy-goldsmith's work, pictorial

61. Badauni, *op. cit.,* p. 236.

62. Payne, *Akbar and the Jesuits,* p. 205.

63. *Ain-i-Akbari,* Vol. I (2nd ed.), p. 169.

act, book-binding, etc., and manufacturing concerns like tapestries, carpet making, curtain making and so forth. Akbar bestowed his personal care and supervision on the work of these workshops. He would pay daily visits to them and watch engineers, manufacturers, artisans and artists at work. Sometimes he would relax and work as an ordinary labourer.[64] He took a special interest in inventing new kinds of guns and other weapons, he fashioned new designs of clothes and shoes and greatly improved the quality of shawls, carpets and woollens.

Akbar every day gave some time to the proper maintenance and welfare of us elephants, horses, camels and other beasts of burden. Their stables were situated very near the royal palaces and a trusted officer of high rank was in charge of them. Akar was particularly fond of elephants and collected the best in the country. They were classified according to their size, quality and value. As for the horses, he took pains to get the best breeds from Kabul, Arabia and other countries of Central Asia. These too were classified according to their breed and qualities, and minute rules were laid down for their care and subsistence. Camels from Ajmer, Jodhpur, Nagaur, Bikaner, Jaisalmer, Bhatinda, and Bhatner were kept in the royal establishments. Similarly, there were a large number of cows and bullocks in the royal studs. Cows from Gujarat were considered the best. The best cows gave half a maund of milk each. There were separate stables for mules, which were employed for carrying the load. Every day Akbar had, according to schedule, some of these animals brought before him for personal inspection. They were given names which Akbar took care to remember. He noted the condition of the animals, asked questions about them, and promoted or demoted their keepers according to the care that they bestowed on them.[65]

Akbar usually held a prolonged meeting of his most confidential advisers during the night. It was an informal assembly, and the members were allowed to sit. Consultations on the most intricate

64. Commentarius, p. 201.

65. *Ain-i-Akbari,* Vol. I (2nd ed.), pp. 123-131.

problems of administration took place and the emperor generally invited the opinions of his advisers and attentively listened to their views. On most occasions, the decisions were those of the emperor, but he asked for the views of all present. After official business, the assembly converted itself into one of learned men, who discussed literature, poetry, religion, philosophy, history, etc. Here books on various subjects were regularly read to Akbar. The meetings continued until midnight when the emperor rose for prayer and sleep. It was at one of these night meetings that Akbar broached the subject of Din-i-Ilahi and persuaded his courtiers to accept his views. The Portuguese missionary Anthony Monserrate who was invited to participate in the discussions has left a graphic account of these nocturnal meetings.[66]

Akbar set apart Thursdays for holding a meeting of the court of justice to try cases, and considered the administration of justice one of the primary duties. On that day there was no formal darbar. At this meeting officers of the judicial department and a few learned ulama were admitted. The emperor usually listened to the appeals from the court of the chief qazi, but sometimes he tried cases in the first instance also. He was very careful in the matter of inflicting punishment, particularly capital punishment. The emperor personally tried all important civil cases and cases involving murder.[67]

Akbar was the first medieval Indian ruler to establish a set of royal institutions and lay down definite rules for the conduct of business by the king. Some of these institutions owed to Akbar their systematisation and others their very birth and evolution. The jharokha-i-darshan was the revival of an ancient Hindu custom which Akbar elaborated in his characteristic manner. Public and private darbars were known to Babur and Humayun. But these were not daily routines with them and were confined to the nobility and the official class. The people had no access to the ruler's court.

---

66. Anthony Monserrate, Commentarius, pp. 180-84.
67. *Ibid.*

There is no mention of regular meetings of diwan-i-am or diwan-i-khas in Babur's memoirs. Nor do the contemporary chronicles of Humayun's reign give a faint indication of their being a regular feature of his administration. There were meetings, pleasure parties, and feasts under these rulers, but no regular daily programme of official work by them through properly established institutions, and hardly any contact between them and the public. The credit for establishing the diwan-i-am and diwan-i-khas as living institutions goes to Akbar. Again, it was Akbar who laid down definite rules for the business to be transacted by the ruler at musters of men and of animals and in the imperial workshops.

The king's daily routine, especially his three open meetings had a profound effect on the general administration, and on the life and conduct of the nobles, officials and the people. The king's appearance before the general public at sunrise was instrumental in stirring up the imagination of the masses and it made a profound appeal to their loyalty. His transaction of business in an open darbar not only brought the king into direct contact with officials but also reduced the chances of domination by any particular minister, officer or clique at the court. And above all, the system thus established by Akbar became a tradition and was followed by his successors till the last days of the Mughal empire.

CHAPTER-III

DEPARTMENTS

The central government consisted of the monarch, who was the pivot of the administrative machinery, and his ministers. The king in ancient India was invariably assisted by ministers who were looked upon as an organic part of the government, Kautilya writes, "Sovereignty is possible only with assistance. A single wheel could never move. Hence the king shall employ ministers and hear their opinion."[68] There were generally speaking three or four ministers, and sometimes their number went up to twelve and even beyond. Of these one was appointed prime minister, another finance minister, and the third was in charge of the portfolio of war and peace. Thus in ancient times ministers had separate departments in their charge. They were required to advise the king either individually or in a body. During the Mauryan times, there was, in addition to the council of ministers, what Kautilya calls the mantri-parishad. R.C. Majumdar gives it the name of State Council as distinguished from the Executive Council[69] which was the Council of Ministers.

The sultans of Delhi, who adopted the administrative system of the Ghaznavides (who had earlier borrowed it from their former overlords, the Samanids of Bukhara), had four ministers.[70] These ministers were the minister of finance (the diwan-i-wazarat),

68. Kautilya, *Arthashastra,* pp. 14-20.
69. R.C. Majumdar, *Ancient India,* pp. 153-55.
70. M. Nazim, *Sultan Mahmud of Ghazna*, p. 130.

the minister of war (diwan-i-arz), the minister of correspondence (diwan-i-risalat), and the minister of espionage (the diwan-i-shughl-i-ishraf-i-mamlukat). The minister of finance generally acted as prime minister and was known as wazir. Besides these four ministers, there was a superintendent of the royal household, who, though not a minister, was as important as and sometimes more important than, the ministers.

During the first few years of his reign, Akbar had only two ministers – a prime minister (vakil), who was in charge of the entire administration, civil and military, and a sadr (head of the ecclesiastical and judicial departments). The prime minister was assisted by a deputy, called the deputy to the prime minister. Pir Muhammad Khan, subsequently entitled Nasir-ul-mulk, was the prime minister's deputy in Bairam Khan's ministry. Shaikh Gadai, a Shia divine, was appointed Sadr by Bairam Khan. There were officers in charge of the army and the finance, but no separate diwan (revenue and finance minister), and probably no bakhshi (or army minister). But sometime after Akbar had taken up the reins of government in his own hands and the administration had evolved to fullness, he had four ministers (excluding deputy ministers), and their number remained constant, throughout his reign. These were the prime minister (vakil), the finance minister (diwan or wazir), the army minister (mir bakhshi), and the minister of ecclesiastical and judicial affairs (sadr).[71]

At one time, however, there were five ministers for a period of nearly two years (1577-1579), when Todar Mal held the post of Mashrif-i-diwan (i.e. super finance minister). But this was an extraordinary thing, and in normal circumstances the number of ministers did not rise beyond four. There was, no mir saman as the head of the household department. There was, however, an officer with the designation of mir saman under Akbar, but he was in charge of court furniture, stores, etc. The royal workshops were

71. *Ain-i-Akbari,* Vol. I (2nd ed.), pp. 4-9.

under a high officer called nasir-i-bayutat, but he did not hold the ministerial rank and worked under the supervision of the finance minister. The finance minister had two deputy ministers under him – diwan of crown (khalisa) territory, diwan-i-tan or one in charge of assigned (jagir) lands. The army minister too had an assistant or deputy minister.

Besides these ministers, there was an advisory council consisting of some twenty members. Akbar frequently consulted the members of this council on important matters, and its meetings were usually held during the night.[72]

Throughout the period of the sultanate of Delhi (1206-1526) the prime minister was called wazir. The word wazir literally means 'a place of refuge' and the wazir was considered an intermediary between the king and the people. There were two kinds of wazirs, one of the first category possessed absolute powers and the other enjoyed only limited authority. The first was commonly called grand wazir, and enjoyed full control over the affairs of the state, whether civil or military. But the wazir of the second category had no power of initiative and only carried out royal orders. Nevertheless, he enjoyed sufficient prestige and possessed greater power and authority than other ministers. Muslim jurists are unanimous of the opinion that non-Muslims are not eligible for appointment as wazir of the first category. Al-Mavardi alone says that a non-Muslim might be appointed wazir of the second category, with limited powers and no initiative of his own.[73]

The Mughal tradition of one wazir with political, financial and military powers in the state, was revived in the early days of Akbar's reign. There were two reasons for it, first, each Babur and Humayun had vakil or grand wazir. Babur's prime minister (vakil) Nizam-ud-din Khalifa, not only enjoyed full powers of government, but he was so powerful that even thought of

72. Anthony Monserrate, *op. cit.*, p. 203.

73. Ibn Hasan, *Central Structure of the Mughal Empire*, pp. 110-117.

regulating the succession to the royal throne. Humayun's prime ministers, Amir Wais, Hindu Beg and Qaracha Beg had held charge of all civil and military affairs.[74] At the time of his accession, Akbar was a mere lad of thirteen and Bairam Khan who became his prime minister was also his tutor and guardian. Therefore, Akbar continued the hereditary tradition of his house, *viz.*, that of having a prime minister (vakil) of the first category with full powers over all departments of administration.

Bairam Khan was the first prime minister of Akbar. He was mainly responsible for the re-conquest of Hindustan in 1555 and was the right-hand man of Humayun. As during the first few years of his reign Akbar remained behind the veil, all the affairs of the state were in his hands. He commanded the army, controlled the finances and appointed and dismissed the highest officers at will. Pir Muhammad, whom Bairam Khan had raised to be his vakil or deputy, conducted the entire administration as if he were not a mere deputy of the prime minister, but a virtual prime minister himself. Such a man was dismissed by Bairam Khan without consulting Akbar, as Pir Muhamad's doorkeeper on one occasion had become guilty of unconsciously slighting the all-powerful prime minister. Bairam's authority can be judged from the fact that he appointed Shaikh Gadai, a Shia divine, to the office of Sadr (the head of the ecclesiastical department) at a Sunni court and in preference to venerated Sayyids. Bairam Khan inflicted capital punishment on inconvenient rivals like Tardi Beg without taking Akbar's orders. He conferred ranks and jagirs and interfered in Akbar's private matters. He was thus a prime minister with unlimited powers and might appropriately be called Grand Wazir.[75]

After the fall of Bairam Khan the prime minister, though he continued to enjoy the original title of vakil, gradually lost unlimited powers of his office, and ceased to be grand wazir in fact, though not in name. As soon as it became known that young Akbar had

74. Babur's Memoirs, Vol. II, pp. 564-565.

75. A.L. Srivastava, *Akbar the Great,* Vol. I, pp. 40-42.

dismissed Bairam Khan, officer after officer hastened to Delhi to join the imperial faction. They were appointed to posts to which they were entitled by their qualifications and ability, by Maham Anaga and Shihab-ud-din Ahmad Khan, leaders of the party, began functioning as de factor prime ministers, and Akbar gladly recognised them as such about the end of March 1560. It may be presumed that the joint prime ministers exercised all the powers and duties of Bairam Khan. But the arrangement did not work, as Maham Anaga was keen to retain her supremacy and make Shihab-ud-din Ahmad Khan and Khwaja Jahan, another powerful leader, her tools. This caused friction and strained her relations with Shihab-ud-din Ahmad Khan to a breaking point, and the latter was consequently removed within a few months.[76] On Maham's recommendation, his place was filled by Bahadur Khan Uzbek, brother of Ali Quli Khan-i-Zaman, as he was the leader of a powerful party at court. This make-shift device also broke down, and after important members of his party had been won over, Bahadur Khan was removed from prime ministership and was transferred to Etawah.[77] Maham Anaga thus recovered her ascendancy and continued to function as prime minister until 10 September 1560 when Munim Khan, a senior official who was recalled from Kabul, was raised to that high office and ennobled with the title of Khan-i-Khanan.[78] A little later he was given Bairam's official residence to live in. But Munim Khan was not a man of outstanding ability, and although he enjoyed full powers of the office, he found it difficult to function without Maham Anaga's cooperation. So he attached himself to the faction of that powerful lady. Nevertheless, his term of office came abruptly to an end after he had functioned for a little over one year, and the post went to the emperor's foster father Atka Khan, whose importunities it was difficult for Akbar to resist.[79]

76. *Ibid.,* pp. 51-52.
77. *Ibid.,* p. 47.
78. *Ibid.*
79. *Ain-i-Akbari,* Vol. II, pp. 112-14.

Shams-ud-din Muhammad Atka Khan was opposed to Maham Anaga.[80] He enjoyed full powers of the prime minister's office and was entrusted with the management of affairs, political and financial, and the disposal of matters relating to the army and to the civil population.[81] The appointment enraged Maham Anaga who regarded herself as the substantial prime minister and Munim Khan who was ostensible vakil and sat on the masnad. These and their partisans, prominent among whom were Shihab-ud-din Ahmad Khan, Qasim Khan and Adham Khan, formed a conspiracy against the new minister and had him murdered in his office in the diwan-i-Khas on 16 May 1562. But Akbar took prompt steps against Maham Anaga's faction and put Adham Khan to instantaneous death. Maham Anaga herself could not survive the shock, and died on the fortieth day of the incident.[82]

The affair was tragic in the extreme. But the young emperor kept his head and displayed tact and political wisdom. Although he had Munim, Qasim, and others who had fled to escape punishment, arrested and brought back to court from their way to Kabul, he forgave them and generously reappointed Munim Khan as prime minister and restored to him his title of Khan-i-Khanan in June 1562.[83] Within a year he appointed a full-fledged revenue and finance minister, and the man (Muzaffar Khan) who was raised to that office was not only unrivalled in his knowledge of finance but was also so independent-minded as not to brook any interference in his department.[84] At about the same time Lashkar Khan was given charge of the military department under the designation of mirbakhshi which had the effect of depriving the prime minister of his military duties and responsibilities as well. Unfortunately, in May 1566, Munim Khan's prestige

80. *Akbar Namah,* Vol. 4, pp. 119-120.
81. *Ibid.,* p. 149.
82. *Ibid.,* pp. 174-177.
83. *Ibid.,* pp. 179-180.
84. *Akbar Namah,* Vol. II, pp. 197-198.

suffered greatly on account of his duplicity in the negotiations with the Uzbek rebels.[85] The prime minister was demoted and sent to Jaunpur to take charge of that province in June 1567. By that time the prime minister of the empire had ceased to be the real controlling authority in court.

After Munim Khan's transfer, Akbar kept the post in abeyance and there was no prime minister for about 6½ years. This was due probably to two reasons. Munim Khan had not been formally dismissed from the prime minister's post, and secondly, no suitable man was available to fill the office. But the empire had grown in size and the work of administration had enormously increased. After the conquest and annexation of Gujarat, it became necessary to revive the office. Therefore, before starting on his triumphal return from Ahmedabad, Akbar issued orders summoning to court, Muzaffar Khan from wherever he could be found. It would be recalled that Muzaffar Khan had incurred the imperial displeasure and was dismissed from the finance minister's post and exiled to Mecca in 1572. Akbar, however, changed his mind within a few months and recalled him from exile. Muzaffar Khan called on the emperor at Fatehpur Sikri, and was appointed prime minister on 18 November 1573.[86] But his term of office as prime minister, though an outstanding success proved to be of very short duration, as he declined to implement Akbar's scheme of fixing the grades of mansabdars, introducing the branding of their horses and of converting the assigned territories (jagir lands) into the Crown (khalisa) lands. Consequently, he was removed from the office within a few months of his appointment.[87]

---

85. *Ibid.*, p. 267.
86. *Ibid.*, Vol. III, pp. 67-68.
87. *Ibid.*, Vol. III, p. 69. Muzaffar remained out of employment for some time. Early in May 1574. Akbar asked him to take charge of the royal camp that was to move to Bihar, but he declined it as derogatory, and so he again fell out of favour.

After a little over three years' gap during which there was no prime minister, Akbar once again invited Muzaffar Khan to fill the post. The latter had for two years rendered valuable military service in Bihar and had repented for his rigid and uncompromising attitude towards some of the imperial projects. He waited on Akbar at Hans Mahal on the latter's way to Ajmer, and was reappointed vakil in October 1577.[88]

The emperor showed him great respect and while he himself and other members of his party got down from their horses and walked one mile to the Khwaja's shrine, he permitted Muzaffar Khan to ride on a led (Kotal) horse of the royal establishment, an honour that was never shown to any prime minister before. Nevertheless, Muzaffar Khan did not exercise full powers of the office and had only nominal control over the finance department, which remained in the powerful hands of Raja Todar Mal and of Khwaja Shah Mansur. They were required to perform their duties in consultation with Muzaffar Khan.[89] Moreover, Muzaffar had little time to restore the original authority of the office even if he had an inclination to attempt what was well-nigh impossible. Akbar was by this time a complete master of all branches of administration and nothing important could be undertaken by the prime minister without his full concurrence and approval. It seems that once again in the highest office of the empire, he failed to come up to the emperor's expectations, either to satisfy him or carry his colleagues with him. That was why Muzaffar Khan's second prime ministership too, like the first one, proved to be of a short duration of one year and a half. On 14 March 1579, he was appointed governor of Bengal and sent there.[90] He took it to be his demotion and accepted the post with reluctance. He remained dissatisfied and did not exert himself to manage the country and the army, and always had the forehead of his heart full of

88. Muhammad Arif Qandhari, *Tarikh-i-Akbar Shahi*, p. 376.
89. *Ain-i-Akbari*, Vol. III, pp. 215-216.
90. *Ibid.*, Vol. III, p. 265.

wrinkles.[91] He filed to control the situation and was slain by the rebels on 19 April 1580.[92]

On Muzaffar Khan's transfer as governor of Bengal in March 1579, Akbar did not appoint any vakil for full two years. The vacancy was filled in March 1582, by the promotion of Todar Mal, who since October 1575 had held the office of Ashraf-i-diwan and had distinguished himself as a soldier and general, a diplomat, and, above all, as a financier. Perhaps the appointment was not made in a formal manner, that is, by investing the raja with the robe of the office and presenting to him the pen case meant for the vakil, as was traditionally done on the occasion of the appointment of a new prime minister. Be that it may, Todar Mal certainly worked as prime minister (vakil) from March 1582 till his death on 8 November 1589. This is clear from Abul Fazl's own words. He writes virtually the position of vakil (prime minister) was conferred on him. Everything was referred to him, and a choice ordering of administrative and financial matters was the result.[93]

It is difficult to say whether Todar Mal enjoyed all the powers of his new office. Ti was against Akbar's considered policy to make his prime minister a de facto head of administration, and consequently the raja must have wielded the powers of a prime minister whom the Muslim jurists call the wazir of the second category. Nevertheless, Akbar gave him his full confidence and turned to him for advice on all important matters. And the raja threw the whole weight of his great ability, extraordinary diligence and loyalty into the work of his exalted office, and proved an eminent success. Abul Fazl, who was not quite happy with him, was constrained to write, "By the blessings of a happy fate Todar Mal sullied not the skirt of wish, but regarded what was good for the state and acquired an ever-lastign good name. With a stout heart he maintained the laws of the caliphate, and had no fear of the powerful and crafty."[94]

91. *Ibid.,* Vol. III, p. 290.
92. *Ibid.,* Vol. III, p. 304.
93. *Ibid.,* Vol. III, p. 381.
94. *Akbar Namah,* Vol. III, p. 381.

Towards the end of October 1589, Todar Mal was at his own request permitted to retire and spend his last days at Hardwar. But he was considered more or less indispensable. Akbar, therefore, rescinded his orders and recalled Todar Mal. But the raja died on 3 November 1589, within a fortnight of his return to duty.[95]

Todar Mal may be said to have been the last great prime minister of Akbar's reign. After his death, the emperor raised Abdur Rahim Khan-i-Khanan to the dignity of prime minister at the end of December 1589. But the new prime minister did not enjoy the real powers of the office. His appointment was a mark of distinction and an act of personal favour. Nevertheless, he continued to remain in the office for about five and a half years. On 19 April 1595 Khan-i-Azam Mirza Aziz Koka, the emperor's favourite foster-brother, was elevated to the post of prime minister.[96] He continued to hold the post till Akbar's death in October 1605. But he too, like the Khan-i-Khanan, did not play any important role in the work of administration. Moreover, as he backed up the candidature of his son-in-law Khusrau in preference to that of the heir-apparent Salim for succession to the throne when Akbar lay confined to a bed of sickness, he must have forfeited the confidence of his dying master.

The history of vikalat or premiership during Akbar's reign was one of gradual decline. The prime minister at the beginning of his reign had enjoyed unlimited authority in political, military, financial and administrative matters. He was gradually sham of all these powers, one by one. At the end of the reign the vakil's post became more or less honorific, and, though he continued to enjoy dignity and prestige, he became a shadow of his former self.

The duties of Akbar's prime minister may conveniently be summarised at this place. The vakil says Abul Fazl, "is the emperor's lieutenant in all matters connected with the realm, and the household. He graces the council by his wisdom, and settles

95. *Ibid.,* p. 363.
96. *Ibid.,* Vol. III, p. 669.

with penetration the great affairs of the realm. Promotion and demotion, appointment and dismissal, depend upon his insight. Although the financial offices are not under his immediate superintendence, yet he receives the returns from the heads of all financial offices, and wisely keeps abstracts of their return."[97]

After Akbar, the position of vakil seems to have gone up. He took all cases for the emperor's orders directly to him. He was consulted by the monarch in almost all important matters, and, though his advice could be ignored, it must have carried weight.[98] Men like Sad-ullah Khan and Himad-ud-Dawlah were fully trusted by their royal masters. He was consulted in all important appointments; practically all fiscal posts were under his patronage. The appointment of the provincial governors and diwans was theoretically within his competence. The officers of the smaller units like the sarkars and the parganahs were also appointed by him in the first instance; they were formally installed with the emperor's approval. He kept strict control over the provincial diwans and their offices and received for scrutiny detailed statements about the income and the expenditure continuously from the provinces. The imperial treasuries also were under his control.

The Wazir controlled the army also when the king was either incompetent or a minor or a pleasure-seeker. The post of wazir was a civil one and it was only in abnormal times that he was expected to perform military duties. On many ceremonial occasions, he acted as the representative of the king. All orders of payments had to be signed by him and all payments were made through his department only. Under the directions of the emperor, he himself passed orders. All questions concerning revenue affairs were settled by him and he consulted the emperor only in important cases. He had two assistants known as the Diwan-i-Am or Diwan of salaries and the Diwan-i-Khas or Diwan of crown lands. After the death of Aurangzeb, wazir became virtually the ruler of the state.

---

97. *Ibid.,* Vol. I (2nd ed.), p. 5.
98. Abdul Hamid Lahuri, *Padshahnamah,* p. 150.

The Diwan (finance minister) is the lieutenant of the emperor in financial matters, superintends the imperial treasuries, and checks all accounts. He is the banker of the cash of the revenue, the cultivator of the wilderness of the world.[99] In short, his main duties were to lay down rules and regulations for the assessment and collection of revenues, to frame the state budget, to allocate funds for the expenditure of various state activities, and to supervise the work of the officers of the department. The mustaufi (deputy diwan), the sahib tawjih (accountant of the army), the awarja-navis) accountant of the daily expenditure of the court), Mir Saman (Officer in charge of court furniture, stores, etc.), the nazir-i-bayutat (superintendent of royal workshops), diwan-i-bayutat (accountant of the royal workshops), the mushrif (superintendent of the treasury) and the amils (revenue collectors) were under his orders and acted by the force of his wisdom.[100]

In the beginning, there was no separate minister for finance during the first few years of Akbar's reign and the prime minister (Vakil) looked after all matters concerning revenue and finance. Soon after taking the reins of government into his own hands, the young emperor decided to reorganize the administration of finance, to take this important work from the hands of the prime minister and continue it into a separate ministry. When Bairam Khan was in disgrace, Akbar raised Khwaja Abdul Majid to the title of Asaf Khan and appointed him wazir sometime about the middle of 1560. But this wazir was not able to reorganize the finance department and his inept handling made confusion worse confounded. He was therefore transferred as the collector of Kara in 1562, and Akbar decided to set the administration of the territory under the direct control of the central government in order. The first step taken in that direction was the establishment of the diwnaship of khalisa (crown) lands. Sometime about the middle of 1562 Aitimad Khan was placed in charge of it under the title of diwan of khalisa. A man of humble origin, the new diwan, had been in his early days in the service of Islam Shah Sur (1545-1554). Akbar recognised

99. *Ain-i-Akbari* (2nd ed.), p. 6.

100. *Ibid.*

his ability, raised him from obscurity and conferred upon him the title of Aitimad Khan. The latter placed the administration of the Khalisa territory on a sound foundation and affected great economy in expenditure.[101] The next step taken, within a year of the creation of diwanship of Khalisa, was the appointment towards the end of 1563 of a full-fledged revenue minister (diwan-i-Kul or wazir) who was placed in charge of both the Khalisa and jagir territories. The department was now completely separated from the prime minister's office (vikalat). This new office was conferred upon Muzaffar Khan Turbati, who had once been in the service of Bairam Khan and had acted successfully, first as the collector of Pasrur (in the Sialkot district) and subsequently as superintendent of imperial stores (diwan-i-bayutat) and had considerable experience of the working of the revenue department.[102] An able financier, though with a head-strong temper, Muzaffar Khan soon acquired power and influence, and it was on his recommendation that Abdun Nabi was appointed Sadr (Minister of ecclesiastical and judicial affairs) in 1565. Under him, the ministry of revenue and finance eclipsed the vikalat. It was Muzaffar Khan's confidential report that brought in 1566 the disgrace of the prime minister Munim Khan and of Khwaja Jahan, the superintendent of treasury and the keeper of the royal seal. This shows that the ministry of revenue and finance had by 1566 become independent of the prime minister and enjoyed equal powers with him. Muzaffar Khan was consulted by the emperor in the matter of appointment of high officials and even ministers. There were at this time four ministers, i.e., prime minister, finance minister, army minister and the minister of ecclesiastical and judicial affairs, and all of these functioned as colleagues. The ministry of finance consisted of two wings, diwan-i-khalisa and diwan-i-jagirs, and both these were under the diwan-i-Kul, i.e., the revenue and finance minister. Since 1562 Aitimad Khan was diwan of Khalisa, but in 1568 Shihab-ud-din Ahmad Khan was appointed to take his place.[103]

---

101. Akbar Namah, Vol. II, pp. 178-179. After Bairam Khan's fall Abdul Majid Asaf Khan and Khwaja Muin-ud-din Farraukhudi were entrusted with revenue and financial matters from 1560 to 1562.
102. *Ibid.,* p. 79.
103. Ibn Hasan, *op. cit.,* p. 151.

During his ministry of eight years and a half (1563-1572) Muzaffar Khan carried out several important financial reforms and greatly consolidated his position and that of his ministry. This was in keeping with Akbar's policy of raising the status of the diwan and abasing that of the vakil. Besides being given charge of finance, he was this time appointed prime minister also. He held the highest office for nearly one and a half years.

In October 1575 Todar mal was appointed Mushrif-i-diwan,[104] a post higher than that of the finance minister but lower than that of the prime minister.[105] In the words of Abul Fazl, "Financial and territorial matters were entrusted to him, and he was made mushrif-i-diwan. He served with honesty and absence of avarice."[106] Although Todar Mal continued in this office, a new finance minister named Khwaja Shah Mansur was appointed in November 1576.[107] Obviously the Khwaja had to work under Todar mal.

Khwaja Abdus Samad Shirin-Qalam was appointed director of the royal mints and given direct charge of the mint at Fatehpur Sikri. The charge of Lahore mint was given to Muzaffar Khan, that of Bengal to Todar Mal, of Jaunpur to Shah Mansur, of Gujarat to Khwaja Imad ud-din of Patna to Asaf Khan. At the same time, an order was issued to mint square rupees.[108] It was during the regime of this ministry that Shah Quli Maharan was removed from the governorship of Punjab on the charge of misgovernment in July 1578 and Said Khan was appointed in his place. Todar Mal was ordered to disperse certain turbulent Afghans who had settled in the towns and villages of Punjab and were oppressing the people. Muzaffar Khan and Shah Mansur were directed to look into the grievances of the people in the territory of Delhi, who had complained against the local revenue officers, and early in 1579.

104. *Ain-i-Akbari,* Vol. III, p. 158.
105. *Ibid.,* p. 6.
106. *Ibid.*
107. *Ibid.,* Vol. III, pp. 193-94.
108. *Akbar Namah,* Vol. III, p. 227.

Muzaffar Khan, Shah Mansur and Qasim Khan were directed to examine the treasury and compare cash with the account books. They found everything in order.[109]

The finance ministry under Todar Mal and Shah Mansur divided the empire into twelve provinces, to each of which a governor (sipahsalar), a diwan, a bakhshi, a mir adl, a sadr, a kotwal, a mir babc (admiral) and recorder (waqaya navis) were appointed.[110] The famous ten-year revenue settlement (ain-i-dahsala) was formulated and enforced.

The prevailing system at that time was to fix assessments every year on the basis of the yield and prices. The result was that the demand of the state varied from year to year. The collectors could not proceed with their work of collection of revenue until the officers fixed the rates to be charged. Todar Mal made a change in the existing system. He got an aggregate of the rates of collection for 10 years from 1570 to 1580 and one-third of them was taken on the basis of assessment. The survey or paimaish of the whole land was undertaken. Formerly, hempen-ropes were used to measure land. The difficulty with them was that they were liable to contract and expand and that resulted in faulty measurement. Todar Mal used a Jarib of bamboos which was joined together with iron rings.

The land was divided into four classes. Polaj land was that land which was regularly cultivated and yielded revenue from year to year. Parauti land was that land which was occasionally left uncultivated so that it may regain its productive capacity during the interval. Chachhar land was that land which was left uncultivated for 3 or 4 years. Banjar land was that land which was left uncultivated for 5 or more years.

The Polaj and Parauti lands were divided into three grades, *i.e.*, good, middling and bad. The average of three was taken as the basis of the assessment. One-third of it was fixed as the share of

109. *Ibid.,* Vol. III, pp. 247-48.
110. *Akbar Namah,* Vol. III, p. 265.

the state. It is to be noted that a different system was followed in the case of Banjar and Chachhar lands. The share of the state was not fixed at one third. The share increased in progressive stages.

Todar Mal fixed rates of converting revenue in kind into revenue in cash by taking an average of the actual prices for ten years. The share of the state was fixed at one third. It was not to fluctuate from year to year. The farmer was given the choice to pay either in cash or in kind.

The chief characteristics of Todar Mal's Bandobast were that the state was to advance loans to the cultivators which could be paid in easy annual instalments. Remissions of revenue were granted in bad seasons. The revenue collectors were required to write officially annual reports about the work, character and integrity of their subordinates. They were to see that cultivators were given a receipt for every payment made by them. A record of all the holding and liabilities of every cultivator was to be maintained. The collectors were to send reports of monthly returns to the royal treasury. Voluntary payments by cultivators were encouraged and the state force was employed only as the last resort. All the Parganas, whether cultivated or not, were required to be measured. Accounts were to be kept in Persian.

The system described above was known as the Zabti system. It was prevalent in Bihar, Allahabad, Lahore, Multan, Delhi, Agra, Awadh, Malwa and parts of Gujarat. Although the ideal administrative system was to be found in the zabti system, there were other systems of assessment prevalent in various parts of the Mughal Empire. The Ghalla Bakshi system was the old Indian system of assessment by the division of crops. It prevailed in Thatta and in parts of Kabul and Kashmir. In the case of the Nasaq system, there was no intermediary between the farmer and the state.

The Mughal government did not give the right of collecting land revenue to the highest bidders. It employed agencies for revenue collection. The Amil was assisted by Bitikchi, Potdar, Qanungo, Muqaddam and Patwari. The Amil was required to examine the registers maintained by the Patwaris, Muqaddams and Karkoons.

The duty of Bitikchi was to supervise the work of the Qanungoes. He was required to be an efficient accountant and a good writer. The Potdar received money from cultivators and issued receipts for all payments. The Qanungo was a Pargana officer. He was acquainted with all rural customs and rites of the peasantry. According to J.N. Sarkar, the Qanungo was "a walking dictionary of the prevailing rules and practices and a store-house of information as to procedure and precedents in the land history of the past.[111]

Khwaja Shami-ud-din was now appointed finance minister on 15 November 1589, and in June next year Qazi Ali Baghdadi was promoted to the post of nazir bayutat. On 12 February 1592, the entire crown territory was divided into four zones obviously to facilitate the revenue administration, and each was placed under an able officer. All the zones continued to function under the new finance minister, Qulij Khan, who seems to have taken over from Khwaja Shams-ud-din in June 1590. In June 1594 collectors of the Khalisa and jagir territories and assayers of the mints were summoned to court and directed to fix weights of the various kinds of coins and their relative values. This work was accomplished under the supervision of Khwaja Shams-ud-din in two months' time. It was an important measure and gave relief to cultivators, traders and others.[112]

In June 1598 another important change was made on the finance department when Rai Tipur Das was raised to the office of diwan at the centre and it was decided that he should work jointly with Khwaja Shams-ud-din. But soon afterwards the Khwaja was transferred to the governorship of the Panjab and Tipur Das became the sole revenue minister of the empire. Tipur Das had hardly worked as finance minister for about a year, when on a report that he took bribes and vexed the people, he was removed from the finance ministry in August 1599 and was sent to deal with the raja of Bhatha, and Asaf Khan II was appointed the diwan-i-kul or full revenue minister.

111. J.N. Sarkar, *Mughal Administration,* p. 50.

112. *Akbar Namah,* Vol. III, p. 570.

The last important change in the finance department was the appointment of Muqim, who was then diwan-i-bayutat to the office of finance minister in place of Asaf Khan, and he was given the title of Wazir Khan. The final step taken by Akbar was the placing of the department of finance under Prince Salim, the heir-apparent. Abul Fazl says, "That the diwans should manage the affairs of the kingdom with the advice of Prince Salim and that his seal should be affixed to the grants of officers mansabs."[113] This was the fitting finale of a series of measures spread over a period of forty years, designed not only to improve the finances of the empire but also to bring them under strict imperial control.

Mir Bakhshi was one of the most powerful officials of the state under the Mughals. He was the army minister and was required to possess literary as well as military qualifications, for besides being in charge of recruitment of troops, their equipment and discipline. He was the paymaster general of the army and had to keep a register of all the mansabdars who were employed on civil or military duties. He was also required to maintain records regarding appointment, promotion, demotion, etc., of all officers. The royal orders regarding the appointment of mansabdars and the grant to them of jagirs passed through his office, and it was his duty to see that they maintained the prescribed number of troops and had their horses branded. The division of the armies into different sections was done in his office, and he had to prepare a list of high mansabdars who were to be in daily attendance on the king. He or his assistant had to be present in formal public darbars and also in the private audience hall in order to place before the king all important matters connected with his department, to introduce candidates for service, to present high officials and visitors, and announce the names of the guards of the palace for rewards. It was his duty to present soldiers and horses for inspection. Sometimes he was required to arrange for the disposition of troops in the field of battle, to lead an expedition as the leader or to command

113. *Ibid.,* Vol. III, pp. 834-35.

a section of the army under a superior captain or general. He accompanied the king on his tours and looked at the arrangements of the royal camp, especially the allotment of places there to the mansabdars.[114]

The first mention of Mir Bakhshi in Abul Fazl's Akbar Namah occurs in connection with the events of March 1565, when Lashkar Khan, who held this post, was sent to Garha to demand from Asaf Khan the war elephants and other valuable bounties that had fallen into his hands in Gondwana. He seems to have been a good soldier, but not a general or organizer of outstanding ability. At any rate, there is no record of his having played a conspicuous role either at court or on the battlefield.

The next notable mir bakshi of the reign was Shahbaz Khan Kambu whose first important employment was as mir tuzuk, i.e., one in charge of royal processions.[115] During Lashkar Khan's eclipse, he seems to have officiated as mir bakshi from July 1571 to September 1572. In this capacity, he accompanied Akbar on the Gujarat expedition in 1572, and after its conquest, he was sent to Ahmedabad to bring the Gujarati nobles, whose loyalty was not above suspicion, to the royal camp. After the battle of Sarnal in December 1572, he was chastised for his negligence on account of which Mahud, son of Sikandar Sur, had succeeded in escaping from his custody and fleeing to the Deccan.[116]

In 1573 Shahbaz Khan was formally appointed mir bakhshi of the empire,[117] and in 1575 he was entrusted with the important administrative duty of enforcing military regulations relating to the reorganization of the army and the branding of horses and of converting the jagir lands into the Khalisa territory.[118] His services in this work seem to have won Akbar's appreciation.

114. Ibn Hasan, *op. cit.*, pp. 215-218.
115. *Akbar Namah,* Vol. II, p. 370.
116. *Ain-i-Akbari*, Vol. III, p. 16.
117. *Muntakhab-ut-Tawarikh,* Vol. II, p. 171.
118. *Akbar Namah,* Vol. III, p. 117.

Shahbaz Khan was an able soldier and general and a successful army minister. He was also a good organizer and administrator. He elaborated military regulations, especially those relating to the system of branding and enforced them rigidly and rapidly. He amassed a large fortune, perhaps not all by honest means, a Karor-worth of which was appropriated by Prince Salim.

The third important mir bakhshi of the reign was Khwaja Nizam-ud-din Ahmad, a renowned historian and courtier. He was at once a first-rate soldier and a balanced scholar. He was the author of the famous Tabat-i-Akbari, a work of great literary and historical merit. The period of his office as army minister was about 2 years and 7 months during which he did not accomplish much. Badayuni however, says that Nizam-ud-din Ahmad won the appreciation of the emperor and acquired an ascendancy at the court on account of his ability, loyalty and diligence, and his balanced approach to problems of administration. He could not see eye with Qulji Khan, the wazir, who had to suffer an eclipse owing to the superior talents of the mir bakhshi.[119]

Shaikh Farid Bokhari, who succeeded Nizam-ud-din Ahmad, was Akbar's last army minister. He was a Sayyid whose ancestors came originally from Bokhara and belonged to a family of religious divines. He took up service under Akbar at an early age and rose to the mansab of 4,000 zat and 2000 sawar. He accompanied Akbar to Kashmir and fought the Kashmir rebel Yadgar. He succeeded in forcing the rajas of Jammu, Ramgarh, Mau, Nagarkot, etc., to acknowledge Akbar's suzerainty. In November 1594 he was appointed mir bakhshi.[120] The most notable work done by Shaikh Farid was to foil the conspiracy against Prince Salim by declining to join Man Singh and Aziz Koka in support of Prince Khusrau and by proceeding to place his entire army at the disposal of the heir-apparent. This prevented a civil war and brought about the

119. *Muntakhab-ut-Tawarikh*, p. 396.
120. *Ibid.*, Vol. II, pp. 396-398.

peaceful accession of Jahangir. Sheikh Farid was an intelligent and able minister.

The army ministers appointed from time to time either to officiate for permanent incumbents or to act in a temporary capacity were Rai Purushottam, Qazi Ali Baghdadi, Jafar Beg Asaf Khan and Khwaja-Ghiyas-ud-din Ali Qazwini. Most of the bakhshis of the reign were soldiers by training and profession.

The mir bakhshi was assisted by two other bakhshis at the centre; he himself was also called the first bakshi; his assistants were called the second and the third bakhshis respectively. In the beginning, one bakhshi was considered adequate to deal with the work, but in Shah Jahan's reign, the number was increased to three. Mostly all the three bakhshis were in attendance in the various audiences of the monarch.[121] The work among them was divided in accordance with the ranks of the mansabdars.[122] The first bakhshi dealt with the royal princes and the highest mansabdars; the second bakhshi dealt with second-grade mansabdars; the third with the lowest. There was a complex procedure for the division of the work regarding the preparation of the various papers and the maintenance of the records; the underlying principle seems to have been that there should be two authorities to check all the entries so that all mistakes should be eliminated. There were, however, some papers which were not considered important enough for this double-check.

The mir bakhshi was kept informed of the main happenings in the provinces by the provincial bakhshis; important items of the news received from them and the Sawanih nigars were reported to the emperor.[123] The bakhshis were responsible for assigning the duty of mounting guard on the palace to the different mansabdars.[124] In the evening when the emperor inspected the guards and the

121. Abd-ul-Hamid, *op. cit.,* pp. 146-47.

122. *Dawabit-i-Alamgiri,* p. 17.

123. Ashraf Khan, *op. cit.,* p. 175.

124. *Diwabit-i-Alamgiri,* p. 18.

royal ensigns were brought out, the bakhshis were in attendance.[125] There was a separate bakshi for the ahadis.[126]

The Sadr (minister of ecclesiastical and judicial affairs) enjoyed great prestige and was indispensable in an Islamic state. By the unanimous verdict of Muslim jurists, one of the principal duties of a Muslim monarch is to protect the shar (Islamic law), to uphold the prestige and dignity of Islam, to follow it in his personal life, and to enforce it in the administration of the country. Then alone he can be called a just monarch (hakim-i-adil) and be entitled to the obedience of his Muslim subjects.[127] According to Ibn Hasan, "The protection of shariat (Muslim Law) has two aspects: the propagation of the knowledge of shar, and its enforcement as a law within the state. The one implies the maintenance of a class of scholars devoted to the study, the teaching and the propagation of the knowledge and the other the appointment of one from amongst those scholars, who is distinguished for learning and piety as an adviser to the king in all his acts of state. The scholars devoted to that knowledge are called ulema (the learned) and the one selected from amongst them is termed Shaikh-ul-Islam.[128] He is also called qazi-ul-quzat (the chief qazi), sadr-i-jahan (chief of the world) or Sadr-us-sudur (chief of the ulema), or simply sadr (chief).

The sadr being the upholder and chief interpreter of the Muslim law and the spokesman of the Muslim theologians (ulema) was the king's adviser in all matters of private or public importance. The king was not only bound to consult him in all matters of law and religion and to follow his advise but also to show him proper respect and uphold his prestige. The sadr had three main duties to perform. First, he was to supervise and control education and to exercise a kind of censorship over the books taught in various educational

125. Kazim, *op. cit.*, p. 1105.
126. Abul Fazl, *Ain-i-Akbari*, p. 105.
127. Al-Mawardi, *op. cit.*, p. 95.
128. Ibn Hasan, *op. cit.*, pp. 255-56.

institutions and over the ideas and morals of the people. He was the representative of the ulema, and it was his duty to bring to the notice of the king what he thought detrimental or prejudicial to the interest of his religion, and the king had little option in acting upon such advice. Secondly, as head of the judicial department, he was responsible for the appointment of qazis, muftis and other judicial officers. In view of this, he had to keep himself in touch with Muslim scholars, as judicial officers were appointed from that class of Muslims only. In fact, he had to ensure a regular supply of Muslim theologians. Thirdly, he was required to dispense a vast royal charity and make recommendations for the grant of jagirs and subsistence allowances. Muslim scholars who were devoted to their religion and learning. He had thus an important place in the administration of the state and was the source of great patronage.[129]

During the first twenty-two years of Akbar's reign, there were four sadrs, and all of them were orthodox Muslims. The first of these was Shaikh Gadai Kambu, a learned Siha divine, who was raised to be the minister of ecclesiastical and judicial affairs by Bairam Khan soon after Akhar's accession in February. He continued to hold the office of sadr until his patron's dismissal in 1560. The Shaikh was a very learned man and also a poet of considerable gift. Both Bairam Khan and Akbar often attended his religious discourses and held him in high esteem. He wielded full powers of bestowing subsistence allowances and grants of land to Muslim divines, scholars and mendicants. He deprived many former recipients, particularly Afghans, of their grants, and bestowed them on those who behaved subserviently and were Shias lie himself.

After the disgrace of Shaikh Gudai, Maulana Abdul Baqi was appointed Sadr, which office he had held during the reign of Humayun. He seems to have worked in this capacity till 1562.[130]

---

129. *Akbar Namah,* Vol. II, pp. 20-21.
130. *Ibid.,* p. Vol. II, p. 114.

Abdul Baqi succeeded in the office of the sadr by Khwaja Muhammad Salih, grandson of Abdullah Mawaridi, early in 1562. He continued to act as minister of ecclesiastical and judicial affairs till 1563-64. But he did not possess independent powers in the matter of grants of jagirs to religious men, without the concurrence of the officers of the revenue department.[131] In religious matters, however, he seems to have wielded full authority. He died in Delhi in June 1598.

Abdun Nabi was the most celebrated sadr of Akbar's reign. On the recommendation of the revenue minister Muzaffar Khan, Akbar raised Abdun Nabi to this office sometime in 1565. The Shaikh continued to work in this capacity till the end of 1578. In the beginning, he enjoyed a great reputation as a scholar and saintly person, and Akbar not only attended his discourses but once or twice reverently picked up the Shaikh's shoes and placed them before his feet. In all matters relating to religion and law and in that of subsistence allowances and religious jagirs Abdun Nabi wielded full authority "when he was appointed sadr-us-sudur", writes, Badayuni, "he distributed enormous areas of land to the people as madad-i-maash, pensions and religious endowments, and never was there in the reign of any monarch, a sadr-us-sudur so powerful as sheikh Abdun Nabi..."[132]

Shaikh Abdun Nabi was in fact very worldly, greedy of money, fond of power, and shallow in learning. Akbar became disgusted with him and when his bribery, mismanagement and rapacity were revealed in an enquiry into the grants of land that he had made, Akbar lost faith in his honesty. In 1579 he was exiled to Mecca, and on return from there without permission, he was imprisoned and placed in the custody of Abul Fazl. He died in prison in 1583. It is said that he was strangled one night.[133]

---

131. *Muntakhab-ut-Tawarikh,* Vol. II, p. 52.
132. *Ibid.,* Vol. III, p. 80.
133. *Ibid.,* Vol. II, pp. 204-08.

Akbar's active interest in the ecclesiastical department began with a discovery of mismanagement and corruption in the grant of subsistence allowances and jagirs. When it was found that Abdun Nabi was greedy, corrupt and unworthy, Akbar decided in January 1578 to curtail his powers and to appoint provincial sadrs, who were to be in charge of land-free-grants and cash allowances in their respective provinces.[134] Within a few months of this decision, he took steps (April-May) to reform the administration of free-grant lands (Sayurghals). Many grantees did not have all their land in one place, and they were harassed by revenue officers and the agents of powerful assignees (jagirdars). Moreover, some grasping persons had encroached upon the Khalisa (royal) territory. Akbar ordered that aima (free grant) land should not be mixed up with Khalisa land or jagir lands, and after a due enquiry into the titles to the grantees, he assigned to each grantee all his land in one place. He also abolished the plurality of situations. Able officers were appointed in every province and district to enforce these reforms.[135] As most of the grantees were found unworthy, those holding 100 bighas or more, if unspecified in their grant deeds, were to lose three-fifths of it. But the Irani and Turani women were exempted from this general rule. All those who had abandoned their old land and taken possession of new land were made to resign one-fourth of it to the state.[136] Early in 1579, Abdun Nabi, who was found guilty of malpractices, was dismissed from the post of sadr. By this time Akbar's views regarding the duties of sadr had undergone a complete change. the ecclesiastical and judicial minister was no longer to be an orthodox Muslim, much less the sheikh-ul-Islam, who could not take long views and did not function for the benefit of the entire Indian community. The emperor was keen that deserving Hindu scholars and religious men should also be made beneficiaries. Hence he decided to

134. *Akbar Namah,* Vol. III, p. 234.

135. *Ibid.,* Vol. III, p. 240.

136. *Ain-i-Akbari,* Vol. I (2nd ed.), p. 279.

appoint a scholar or tolerant views to this office. In the words of Abul Fazl, "As the circumstances of men have to be inquired into before grants are made, and their petitions must be considered in fairness, an experienced man of correct intentions is employed for this office. He ought to be at peace with every party, and must be kind towards the people at large in word and action."[137] In view of this Sultan Khwaja, a liberal Musalman and a member of the Din-i-Ilahi, who had recently returned from Mecca, was appointed sadr in January 1579 and was given the title of Turkhan.[138]

In October 1581 Akbar further curtailed the powers of the chief sadr and appointed honest and experienced men to look after the administration of free-grant lands of the empire. For this purpose, the empire was divided into six zones with a sadr in charge of each. The provinces of Delhi, Malwa and Gujarat were placed under Hakim Abul Fath, those of Agra, Kalpi and Kalinjar under Shaikh Faizi, the country from Hajipur to the Sarju under Hakim Humam, Bhiar under Hakim Ali, Bengal under Hakim Ain-ul-mulk and the Panjab under Qazi Ali Bakhshi.

Sultan Khwaja died at Fatehpur Sikri on 2th July, 1584, and Mir Fath-ullah Shirazi was appointed to succeed him. But as he was sent on political missions to the Deccan, the duties of the Sadr's office devolved on his assistant, named Kamal. The powers of the sadr suffered further diminution. On Mir Fath-Ullah Shirazi's death in August 1589, sadr-Jahan was appointed Sadr. He was a member of the Din-i-Ilahi and consequently a man of liberal and tolerant views. Akbar continued to take a personal interest in the work of the department. The Irani and Turani women, who had been formerly exempt from the general rule governing the grant of sayurghals, were also found guilty of fraud and, therefore, all those women who were found in possession of more than 100 bighas of land were made to surrender the excess of 100 bighas. When Mir Fath-ullah

137. *Ibid.,* Vol. I (2nd ed.), p. 278.
138. *Akbar Namah,* Vol. III, p. 263.

Shirazi was sadr, Akbar directed that he should not grant more than 15 bighas of land without the emperor's permission.

Akbar's unfailing interest reformed and remodelled the ecclesiastical department in some important particulars. In the first place, the sadr ceased to be the head of the ulema and the chief interpreter of the Muslim law. He no longer exercised effective moral control over the emperor's private life and over his religious opinions and conduct, and his authority to grant subsistence allowances, which were not thrown open to deserving men of all religions, was reduced considerably. Secondly, the organisation of the ulema, which had for centuries thriven on state bounty, was broken up and made to lose its aggressive character. Thirdly, most of the old-type qazis (judges), who were found corrupt, were dismissed and their places were given to abler men of tolerant views. Fourthly, the interests of the state were served by the reduction of the number and value of indiscriminate grants of land. And finally, the appointment of provincial and city sadrs not only made the administrative machinery of the department more elaborate and sound, but it also brought the individual grantees of land for subsistence purposes into more intimate contact with the government and minimized the chances of corruption.

Akbar had, besides his ministers, an advisory council of twenty members who were senior courtiers and did not necessarily hold any definite office in the state service. It was a novelty in medieval Indian administration, for no Muslim ruler of India before Akbar had such an institution. It was an informal assembly presided over by the emperor, or sometimes a senior noble or official nominated for the purpose and its meetings were held usually during the night. Akbar held consultations with it on momentous matters of war and peace. Sometimes he rejected the unanimous decision of the council, if it did not appeal to him. A European eyewitness says, "Akbar has about twenty Hindu chieftains as ministers and counselors to assist both the work of governing the empire and in the control of the royal household. They are devoted to him and are very wise and reliable in conducting public business. They are always with him and are admitted to the inner-most parts of the palace, which is a privilege not allowed to the Mughal nobles."[139]

Although not technically a department of the state the imperial household was in actual practice administered as a separate state department and was larger and more important than any department of central administration, for it concerned the emperor and the members of the royal family directly and it was on their safety, good health and comfort that the entire administration depended. It was not included in the charge of any minister, and there was no high officer like the Khan-i-Saman or Mir Saman of the later times as its head. It was the emperor's personal responsibility to look after its administration, and Akbar took great interest in the management of the several institutions that comprised the royal household. In 1583 he established a small board consisting of Rai Sal Darbari, Kara mullah, Khwaja Abdus Samad and Muhammad Ali Khazanchi and presided over by Prince Murad, to help him in discharging this responsibility.[140]

The core of this department was the royal harem which consisted of more than 5,000 women, each of whom was given a separate apartment to reside in. some of these women were the emperor's wives, many of them were his relatives, and a very large number consisted of all kinds of servants, such as maid-servants, clerks, ladies-in-waiting, physicians, nurses, midwives, armed retainers, and so forth. The harem was located inside a large enclosure and had numerous fine buildings. The ladies' apartments were divided into sections, and women darogas or superintendents were appointed over each section.[141]

---

139. *Commentarius,* pp. 203-204.
140. *Akbar Namah,* Vol. III, p. 404.
141. *Ain-i-Akbari,* Vol. I (2nd ed.), p. 46.

The inner enclosure of the harem was guarded by women soldiers, and the most trustworthy among them were posed around the apartments of the emperor. Eunuchs were posted outside the enclosure, and at some distance, faithful Rajputs were stationed all around as reliable guards. At the gates of the imperial palaces were posed porters whose duty was to keep watch on all who came in or went out of the palaces. Nobles, ahdis and other troops were posted on all sides of the palaces. Abul Fazl says, "Not withstanding the great number of faithful guards, his Majesty does not dispense with his own vigilance, but keeps the whole in proper order".[142]

A capable writer or accountant, probably with some assistants, was appointed to look after the expenditure of the harem. The imperial ladies had fixed salaries or allowances, and those of the highest among them ranged from Rs. 1028 to Rs. 1610 per month. Besides, they were given costly presents by the emperor from time to time. The salaries of the women servants ranged from Rs. 20 to Rs. 51 a month. Maid-servants were paid at the rate of Rs. 2 per mensum, and important among them received Rs. 40 per month. The writer in charge of the harem was entrusted with accounts and stores, and supervised the expenditure.

The imperial kitchen was an elaborately organized institution. Its head, called mir bakawal or master of the kitchen, was a highly trusted and vigilant officer, and worked under the general supervision of the prime minister. Under him, there were a number of sub-bakawals. There were also treasurers for cash and for stores, a number of tasters and an able and efficient accountant. The numerous cooks hailed from the various parts of the country and were specialists in charge of preparations of a great variety of dishes, vegetarian and non-vegetarian. As with other departments, an annual budget for the expenditure of the kitchen was prepared at the beginning of every year. For the purpose of collecting and

142. *Ibid.*, p. 47.

storing up the commodities required for the kitchen the year was divided into two parts or seasons, and at the beginning of each season, the diwan-i-bayutat and mir bakawal collected the commodities. We have a detailed account of the best kind of rice, wheat, ghee, fowl, etc., and places from where these were procured.

A large variety of dishes, several hundred in number, was prepared every day and these were served in plates of gold and silver, stone and china-ware. After a set of dishes was ready, they were tasted by the cooks and the bakawal concerned, and when all the dishes were ready they were tasted by the mir bakawal before being served to the emperor. In the palace, these were again tasted by the royal servants, and then arranged on the table cloth. These elaborate arrangements were precautions against poisoning.[143]

The drinking water was in the charge of a trusted officer, and the institution was called abdar khana. Whether at home or on tours Akbar drank water from the Ganga. Several dozens of persons were employed to bring the Ganga-water in sealed jars. But after 1586 when Akbar made Lahore his seat of residence for several years, the water from the Chinab was brought for cooking purposes, and the Ganga-water was brought from Hardwar.[144]

The members of the imperial household and of the court made use of ice-cold water during summer. The cooling was done by an ingenious process with the help of a saltpetre. But when the royal court moved to Lahore in 1586, snow and ice were brought from the district of Panhan in the northern mountains about 90 miles from Lahore. We are told by Abul Fazl that all ranks used ice in summer, and the nobles used it during all seasons.

Another institution under the household department was the wardrobe and the stores for mattresses. Numerous kinds of clothes and dresses for the use of the emperor were kept in the wardrobe. They were classified and arranged according to their qualities and

143. *Ibid.,* pp. 60-61.
144. *Ibid.,* p. 58.

prices. Akbar sometimes put on European (particularly Portuguese) clothes, and sometimes Persian and Mongolian dress, besides the usual Indian costume which he used daily. One thousand complete suits for the imperial wardrobe were prepared at the beginning of every season, and one hundred and twenty suits, arranged in twelve bundles were always kept in readiness. During winter Akbar preferred woollen stuff, especially the shawls. There were various kinds of turbans, plain, coloured and ornamented. Like the Hindus, Akbar tied the strings of his coat on the right side and not on the left side which was the practice of the Muslims.

Another important institution under the household department was the imperial farrash khana. Akbar was fond of outdoor life and was often on tours. It was, therefore, necessary to have good camping arrangements and such strong and serviceable tents as could afford protection from the sun and the rain. With his characteristic zeal for organisation and improvement, Akbar introduced many important changes to the royal tents and furniture. Abul Fazl says, "the department has been much improved both in the quality and quantity of the stores, and also by the introduction of new fashions."[145]

The main royal camp was called bargah which was of various sizes. The largest bargah was able to accommodate more than 10,000 people. It was so large and heavy that it took a thousand skilled labourers a week to erect it with the help of machines. Another tent was called chubin raoti, and was raised on tem pillars. The third tent was called doashiyana manzil. It was a tent of two storey and was erected on 18 poles, six yards in height. Another tent was called Zamindoz or a tent of various forms with either one or two doors.

It would not be out of place to give a brief account of Akbar's encampment during his tours and military expeditions. The encamping ground covered several miles in area. Round the

145. *Ibid.*, p. 55.

imperial camp was erected a grand enclosure called gulabar which consisted of strong wooden planks and the doors of which were secured with locks and keys. The gulabar was at least 100 square yards. Outside the gulabar there were erected tents for the nobles and servants.

Monserrate gives a life-like picture of Akbar on the march. Royal guards marched behind the emperor at a stone's throw, and the party proceeded in a crescent-shaped formation. The distance covered was measured every day by a ten-foot-long rod was duly accorded in the daily diary.[146]

Attached to the household department was a school for Akbar's sons and grandsons. Other children connected with the royal family and those of the emperor's relations were also admitted to the school. As usual, the school-going ceremony of a child took place when he had reached the age of 4 years 4 months and 4 days, and the initiation ceremony was performed at an auspicious hour. The princes were given literary as well as military education. They were taught Persian, Turki, Hindi and something of Arabic. The military training of the princes included riding, racing, commanding of troops and handling of weapons of offence and defence. "The princes", writes Monserrate, "have also trainers to teach them the use of arms, riding masters and instructors in archery."[147]

It may be mentioned at this place that Akbar had a magnificent library consisting of 24,000 manuscript books on various subjects, such as fiction, history, philosophy, theology and sciences. There were in addition Persian translations of many valuable Sanskrit, Arabic and Greek works. A number of officers and servants were employed to keep the library in excellent working order. The imperial library must be considered an institution of great value attached to the household department.

146. *Commentarius*, pp. 78-79.
147. *Ibid.*, p. 199.

There was no separate department of royal conveyances, as the army had a large number of elephants, horses, camels and other transport animals and these were at the disposal of the royal family. When a boy in Kabul, Akbar was personally very fond of riding camels, but in India, he took fancy for elephants and took delight in controlling and riding the most ferocious elephants and horses. But sometimes he drove in a carriage. There were bullock carriages, called bahals. Some of these carriages were four-wheeled ones, and were pulled by two or more bullocks.[148] Akbar travelled in a *rath* (horse or camel cart) on his journey to Gujarati in 1573.[149] Monserrate writes, "Akbar drives a two-horse chariot in which his appearance is very striking and dignified."[150]

There was a small department of feasts and fancy bazaars. The fancy-bazars day was called Khusroz (day of enjoyment). The fancy bazaars were held on the third feast-day of every month when women were permitted to put up stalls of various fancy articles. The bazaars were visited by the ladies of the imperial harem, and the wives of nobles and officers too were invited to attend them. There were fancy bazaars for men too. Merchants from many countries brought to sell their wares at these marts. There was a separate staff appointed for the transaction of business on behalf of the emperor in the fancy bazaars.

The department of the royal hunt was under an officer called mir shikar or master of hunting. Special rules were laid down for imperial hunting expeditions. More than one officer was employed to keep a vigilant eye and guard the hunting ground. Only those officers were allowed to go near the emperor as were required to render service at the chase. Minute rules were laid down for tiger hunting of which Akbar was very fond. Another pastime was elephant-catch in which

148. *Ain-i-Akbari,* Vol. I (2nd ed.), p. 265.
149. A.L. Srivastava, *Akbar the Great,* Vol. I, p. 148.
150. Monserrate, *op. cit.,* p. 199.

he took a personal interest. Leopard hunting came only third and thereafter hunting of other wild animals.

There were other forms of royal amusements. Next to hunting was the game of polo or chaugan. Another pastime of Akbar was pigeon flying, in which he retained interest till his old age. The emperor took part in indoor games like chaupar, playing cards, chess, etc. There were separate officers in charge of these games.[151]

The naqqar khana or music gallery was an important royal institution and was attached to the household department. It was located on the upper storey of the gateway or entrance to the royal palaces. Besides its value as one of the royal prerogatives, the naqqar khana kept the people informed of the emperor's daily routine and activities with beat of drum and allied music. The surna began to be played about half an hour before sunrise. Thereafter insie was played at fixed hours several times during the day and night.[152]

There were more than a hundred workshops, and these were situated in the towns of Lahore, Agra, Fatehpur Sikri, Ahmedabad and Gujarat and in some other parts.[153] Each workshop was concerned with the manufacture of a special article. Some of them were meant exclusively for the manufacture of guns of various calibres and weapons needed for the army. Each workshop resembling a city or rather a little kingdom was under an officer who possessed special knowledge of the commodity or article which it manufactured. There were accountants, writers, and men of various other descriptions attached to the workshop. The entire organisation was under the diwan-i-bayutat who functioned under the emperor's supervision.

At the beginning of Akbar's reign, the imperial secretariat and the offices of all the four ministers were situated inside the

151. *Ain-i-Akbari*, vol. I (2nd ed.), pp. 292-320.
152. *Ibid.*, pp. 52-53.
153. *Ibid.*, p. 12.

fort at Agra, and when Akbar transferred his residence to Fatehpur Sikri, these officers were located within the enclosure of the royal palaces. Important political and financial matters were placed before him and acted upon according to his orders. His signatures were obtained on important documents. This system continued for some years more with the state hall forming the nucleus of the secretariat. Referring to the secretariat as it was in 1580 the Jesuit writer Monserrate says, "The crowd of officers, secretaries and pay-masters, who administer the royal supplies, and grant safe conducts, passes, contracts, etc., are accommodated in a very large hall. This secretariat is presided over by a chieftain of great authority and ability who signs the royal farmans."[154]

A hospital was attached to the palace. Abul Fazl gives the names of more than two dozen of famous physicians and surgeons. Hakim Misri, Hakim Abdul Fath Gilani and Hakim Ali were front rank physicians and the most notable among them was Hakim Misri who was called "the Galen of the age". He had a unique knowledge of external and spiritual matters. He had such a knowledge of medicine that if medical books had disappeared he would have written them out from memory. Two other physicians celebrated throughout India were Narayan Mishra and Bhim Nath. The most notable surgeons were Shaikh Bina and Shaikh Hansu.[155] In 1582 hospitals were established in different parts of the empire.[156]

---

154. *Commentarius,* pp. 208-209.

155 *Ain-i-Akbari,* Vol. I, p. 613.

156 *Ibid.,* Vol. III, p. 380.

CHAPTER IV

NATURE OF THE CENTRAL ADMINISTRATION

It is now generally conceded that Akbar's administration owed a great deal to Sher Shah, hence the point need not be laboured any further. It is unnecessary to argue that the administration institutions of the Mughal empire were mostly a continuation of the administration of the sultanate with some alterations and improvements, which form the subject of this chapter.

The changes began to be introduced by Akbar and the concluding date has been fixed at 1707 when Alamgir I died and the Mughal empire began to disintegrate rapidly. The administrative institutions did not die suddenly. With the increasing weakness of the central authority they gradually lost their vigour and many of them were swept away by the flood of anarchy that engulfed the land destroying the patient work of several centuries. Yet, all was not lost, because at the provincial and local levels wherever some authority continued to exist, many of the old institutions survived. Some of them were taken up by the British who supplanted the Mughals.

The Mughal period differs from the Sultanate in one important respect. During these one hundred and fifty-one years it was one dynasty that ruled the realm. It is true that the death of a monarch was often a signal for civil war, but the contestants were scions of the same family. And they fought for themselves: they were not puppets in the hands of ambitious nobles. The nobles allied themselves with princes of their choice in whose service they hoped to attain their own objects, but the nobles themselves were not aspirants to the throne itself. The prestige of the family was so well-established that no outsider could dream of questioning its sole right to provide the monarch. Even when, after 1707, the power of the emperor declined and some princes were merely puppets in the hands of ambitious disruptionists of imperial authority, the right of the dynasty to reign over the realm was not questioned, so much so that when the Marathas and the British usurped imperial authority, they continued to rule in the name of the great Mughal. It was only after the power of the Muslims had been sufficiently broken that the British decided to do away with the pretence of Mughal sovereignty.

Several factors contributed to the success of the Mughals in establishing their dynasty so firmly. The Sultanate had existed in stormy times. The Mongol inroads had unsettled the world of Islam. The Sultanate could not afford the luxury of dynastic stability because it needed strong men of action to meet the challenge. When, with the conversion of the Mongols to Islam and their adoption of civilized ways, the challenge seemed to weaken, it did not result in accession to the strength of any dynasty. It only produced disintegration. Provincial dynasties prospered, but Delhi itself fell prey to discord and conflict. In any case, the feeling that the danger had disappeared was only a delusion.

By the time Akbar established himself firmly, a balance of power emerged in central Asia. The Mughals, the Safawis and the Uzbegs were well established and each one of these was suspicious of the intentions of the other two. The Safawis had discovered, as the Mughals were to discover later, that a central Asian adventure was not paying. The Uzbegs had been punished severely by the Safawis when Shaibani Khan and Shah Ismail had tried their strength. The Mughals had a wholesome respect for the Safawis as well because of their experience in Qandhar which they finally lost to Iran in

1653. The Mughals exercised considerable vigilance and were rewarded by the disinclination of their neighbours to undertake an invasion of their territories. The respite from external invasions was a source of great strength to the Mughals, because all their resources could be diverted to the conquest of the subcontinent and the consolidation of their power.

The establishment of the mansabdari system, which gradually eliminated tribal chiefs as nuclei of power and possible intrigue, and its successful working made it possible for the emperor to assert himself more fully. The tribal element was not completely eliminated. For instance, the Rajput nobles had a large number of ancestral adherents and a quasi-feudal system to back them. Yet such elements were counter-balanced by others. Through the mansabdari system, the habit of looking upon the emperor as the source of all advancement and honour came to be established, which grew into a strong tradition. The Mughals successfully adopted the stratagem of balancing one group against another and making each one dependent upon themselves.

Yet another factor was that under the Sultans of the Muslim population, surrounded by danger on all sides, was aware of the need for strong men to defend it from external invasion and local rebellions. It realized the importance of successful generals and was in no mood to tolerate weaklings, even though they might have a better claim to the throne. With the employment of a much larger number of Hindu generals and soldiers under the Mughals, this reliance upon the Muslim warriors was weakened and its place was taken by a dependence upon the emperor who controlled the warriors and their leaders. It was for this reason that the Muslim masses were lulled into a false sense of security and awoke to the stark reality of the loss of political power when it was too late. It was to deceive then from that the Marathas and the British had alike made a pretence of deriving their authority from the emperor.[157]

---

157. I.H. Qureshi, *The Administration of the Mughal Empire*, pp. 4-5.

The good government that the Mughals gave their empire was no small factor in winning the affection of the people. As the entire administration was centred on the monarch who looked into every detail himself, his person came to embody the hopes of peaceful existence, justice and prosperity. The Mughal ideals of benevolence, justice and good government secured stability for their dynasty.

The most important factor, however, was the ability of the dynasty to produce, is the course of a century and a half, four capable men who understood the problems of their government and had the energy to enforce their policies. The only period in which the monarch was not able to devote all his attention was when, during his last years, Jahangir's health broke down. His ministers, however, maintained their grip on the administration. The dynasty was served by some good ministers. Several names like those of Itimad-ud-Dawlah, Sadullah Khan and Mir Jumla stand out for their efficiency and wisdom.

Some writers have painted Jahangir as a besotted drunkard who cared little for the affairs of the state and even less for Islam. This picture is grossly unfair to the monarch. It can be easily proved that he took an active interest in the administration of his empire so long as his health remained sound. It was only during the last few years, when his health broke down, that his active interest decreased and the administration was carried on by others. Similarly, in matters of religion, he was a believing Muslim and supported the cause of orthodoxy. His tolerance of other faiths was misunderstood by foreigners like Sir Thomas Roe as unbelief because in their own lands they were not used to such broadmindedness. They could not understand that a believer need not be intolerant.

Jahangir did not forget his own feelings when his father had failed to accord due recognition to his position as the heir apparent. He, therefore, bestowed the title of Shah Jahan on Prince Khurram and gave him the unprecedented rank of thirty thousand. However, when the government came under the influence of Nur

Jahan, she created difficulties for Shah Jahan who was left with no choice but that of rebellion, which was crushed and it seemed that his chances of ever regaining sufficient power to contact the succession had been irretrievably damaged. However, at the crucial time, through the support of his father-in-law, Asaf Khan, he succeeded in defeating Nur Jahan's nominee Sharyar, who had no talent for ruling.

Jahangir did not introduce any remarkable reforms in the administration. Efforts to bring about improvement are on record. The monarch's benevolent nature found an expression in trying to secure for the people a just and well-run administration. He was a great patron of painting in which he had a refined and cultivated taste. Under him, the Mughal school of miniature painting reached the zenith of its progress.

Shah Jahan's reign has been rightly looked upon as the golden age of the Mughal empire. Until the beginning of the war of succession, there was peace in the realm. A great wazir, Sad-ullah-Khan ran the administration with prudence and ability. A number of changes were brought about in the administrative institutions. This brought about a visible increase in general prosperity, which is reflected in the architectural achievements of the reign. Mughal architecture reached the climax of its excellence under Shah Jahan who gave posterity buildings like the world-famous Taj Mahal, the Jama Masjid of Delhi, the exquisite Pearl Mosque of Agra and the romantic pavilions of the palace-fortress, Lal Oilah of Delhi. It is about these buildings that it has been said that the Mughals built like Titans and finished like jewellers. In this reign red sandstone was replaced by marble and tessellation by pietra dura. The same impression of richness is conveyed by the introduction of gold and gold ornamentation in the miniatures and manuscripts. Life was characterized by unparalleled elegance and luxury. The splendour of the imperial and provincial courts under Shah Jahan dazzled all foreign visitors, whether Asian or European.

When Alamgir came to the throne, forces of decay began slowly to assert themselves. Indeed the reign of Shah Jahan gives to the historian the impression of ripe fruit ready to fall from the tree at the first gust of the mind. It sprang up like a gentle breeze under Alamgir I and then developed into a hurricane. The centrifugal forces, always present in the political life of the subcontinents, began to raise their head in the form of rebellions and disorders. In the beginning, it was not difficult to deal with them. The Maratha trouble, however, was of a different nature. The Marathas had been employed as hardy and useful soldiers by early Muslim rulers, but with the decline in the power of the rulers of Bijapur and Golconda, they discovered that defiance of authority, after all, was not too difficult.

The ambitious Shivaji, the son of a trusted noble of Bijapur court, found brigandage and rebellion more profitable than service of the state. This was the beginning of the avalanche that destroyed the Mughal empire and plunged the subcontinent into anarchy for more than a century. Alamgir I is credited with fighting the storm with great courage and determination. He almost succeeded in overcoming it. He might have succeeded if he had been supported by his officers more loyally and if his policies had been followed by his successors. But corruption and treachery stalked in his camp and after his death, some selfish nobles made common cause with the Marathas, thus digging the grave of Muslim rule in India.[158]

Alamgir showed his administrative acumen while anarchy had yet not drawn him and his forces into its vortex. Despite the tremendous drain on the resources of the empire and his military preoccupations, he did not permit his administration to fall prey to disorganization or disintegration. Indeed the prosecution of a prolonged and expensive war would have been impossible but for the proper functioning of the administration. It was not the administration alone that suffered. Both architecture and

---

158. *Ibid.*, p. 9.

painting succumbed and though some good buildings like the Padshahi Mosque at Lahore and scores of paintings of Alamgir's reign have come down to us, they do not hold a mirror to Shah Jahan's contribution.

The Mughal empire was de jure as well as de facto an independent state. The emperor, styled as padshah, was recognised as the Caliph within his realm. He, therefore, owed no allegiance to the Ottoman Caliph who claimed to have inherited the mantle from the Abbasid Caliphs of Egypt. He was, however, subservient to shar, the Muslim law and had no authority to amend or annul it. It so happened that Jahangir restored the institutions of orthodoxy and Shah Jahan and Alamgir I were pious and orthodox monarchs.[159]

Justice and hisbah were organised on traditional orthodox lines. The administration of justice was divided into three categories: Siyasat, mazalim and qada. The first dealt with military and political offences, the second with cases arising out of the dealings of public prevents with the public, and the third with ordinary criminal and civil suits. These courts were differently organized. Qada hisbah and religious affairs were under the sadr-us-sudur who was also the supreme judge of the empire and in this capacity was called quaji-ul-qujat. The mir-adl dealt with executive matters relating to justice like the production of litigants in the courts and implementing their orders.

The provincial government was modelled on the lines of the central government. The various departments were reproduced and directly corresponded with their central counterparts under whose general direction they worked. The head of the provincial government was the sipah-salar who later came to be called subahdar. The local government was primarily based in the parganah which was a collection of villages. The parganah was under an amil who was mainly concerned with revenue matters. Between the parganah and the province were interposed sarkars

159. *Ibid.*, p. 11.

under Faujdars whose main duty was the maintenance of peace. The sarkar was for some time an administrative unit as well.

As the Shar does not envisage hereditary monarchy, it provides no law of succession for monarchical dynasties. The law hold on tenaciously to the principle of election, but it was generally believed that there was no bar to the succession of a son to the throne of his father. This was a compromise with the position created by the establishment of dynasties in the Muslim world. There were several precedents among the Mughals when territories were virtually divided among several sons: sometimes princes went on contending for power and thrones, the fact of the rebellion being treated rather lightly. Babur had to fight for his heritage from a very early age, Humayun was faced with the opposition of all his brothers at one time or another. Only too often did he forgive his brothers and ultimately Kamran, the arch rebel, was blinded and exiled, which, judging by his long record of rebellion and fighting against his brother was not such an extreme measure, because his life was spared. The other brothers who also had rebelled and proclaimed themselves emperors on various occasions were leniently treated. Akbar's brother, Hakim, who had marched against the emperor at a critical time in his reign to contest the imperial throne was forgiven, Salim's rebellion was not serious; it was petulant behaviour to draw Akbar's attention to the fact that the prince had grown into a mature man which needed some recognition. At the time of his father's death, Salim had a serious competitor for the throne in his son Khusrau who could not reconcile himself, even after Salim's accession, to have to wait for the crown. Khurram's way to the throne also was littered with difficulties which had been created by Nur Jahan and her party. The war of Succession which led to Aurangzeb's enthronement involved almost the entire empire in war and led to a considerable weakening of the administrative machinery. When he was able to establish his power Aurangzeb, now Alamgir, had to take special measures to restore the economic life of the empire and its administrative efficiency.[160] The climax, however, came after Alamgir I's death. His sons had prepared too long and the result would be more a matter of resources than personal character. Alamgir I was fully aware of the consequences of such a war and he tried to persuade his sons to agree to a division of the empire.[161] They did not agree. The empire bled by the long war in the Deccan. Gradually the empire lost all power but never lost up to its final extinction, the tradition of rivalry among the princes for the throne. Nothing contributed so much to its final dissolution as the absence of any recognized principles of succession.

The Mughal empire provided a real need in filling up the vacuum in political power after the weakening of the Delhi Sultanate. It started on its career of glory under Akbar and fell to pieces soon after Alamgir I. Babur's initial victories had shown the military decadence of the sultanate; Humayun's easy conquests of Gujarat and Malwa had demonstrated further that the other kingdoms of the subcontinent also were no better. It was Shershah's military and political genius which took advantage of the divisions in the Mughal camp and succeeded in turning out the Mughals: but after his death, the chronic divisions among the Afghans recrudesced until Humayun was able to come back. Then began the historic mission of the Mughal empire to give peace and good government to the country which had been torn by internecine warfare. The Mughals created confidence and by following their ideal of benevolent and paternal government won the respect of the people. The empire achieved almost a sanctity. Even when the forces of anarchy succeeded in depriving the emperor of all his power, they took considerable time to reduce his prestige. Sindhiya held Emperor Shah Alam as a puppet and granted him so meagre an allowance that the court was almost starving and in tatters; and his master Peshwa received the imperial grant of appointing him the vicegerent of the empire with a great ceremony

160. Kazim, *op. cit.*, p. 438.
161. Ashraf Khan, *op. cit.*, p. 7.

attended with public rejoicing and Sindhiya himself was proud of having been appointed the deputy vicegerent. The British officers signed themselves as servants of Emperor Shah Alam although the company would not pay him a pie out of the revenues of the land which they ostensibly administered for him. The need to hide the political reality under a legal myth arose from the fact that the empire was too deeply enshrined in popular affection to make it good policy to proclaim that its authority had been usurped. To the Muslims, the emperor was a symbol of their sovereignty, to the non-Muslims, of ordered and benevolent government. It is not surprising that the myth propounded by Abul Fazl that royalty was a ray of Divine Light, though un-Islamic in spirit and transgressing the Hindu ideas of exclusiveness, found a place in popular belief.

The Mughals have seldom been surpassed in the elegance and splendour of their court. They knew fuil well the psychological importance of maintaining the dignity of the monarchy, and they cultivated manners of speech and modes of behaviour which would not compromise it. Under the influence of their court came into existence a style of writing which could express the harshest sentiments in the political language. The mellowness and elegance expressed in their architecture also pervaded their mode of living which had been cultivated almost into fine art. All that was harsh and unpleasant was gradually eliminated, until at last the grit which makes soldiers and administrators ebbed out of the society which accepted their standards. The Mughal imperial family never lost its traditions of bravery, but little stamina was left in their followers and supporters.

The splendour of the Mughal court almost defies description. The marble halls of the fortress palaces of Agra, Delhi and Lahore, overwhelming in beauty and dignity even today, are yet mere shells; when their builders held court in them, they were hung with the richest carpets and cloth mostly embroidered with gold; the canopies were made of rich materials supported by posts cased in gold or silver, the dresses of the officers were of silks interwoven with threads of precious metals or embroidered with gold...[162] The same splendour was maintained in royal processions and journeys.

The Mughals were extremely jealous in the matter of the respect which they thought was due to them, and severely reprimanded any failure on the part of a noble to show due to humility or any assumption of prerogatives or customs by him which did not conform with the Mughal ideas of the limitations imposed by the protocol upon a subject.[163] Even powerful vassals like the rulers of the Deccan States were not spared.[164]

The royal Imperial household set the fashion for other dignitaries as well. The princely Viceroy, the governors the hereditary Hindu princes and other high officials maintained establishments which within their capacity, were modelled upon the pattern of the imperial household. The Mughal patterns of polite behaviour came to be accepted all over the subcontinent and continued to influence notions regarding etiquette and good manners long after the empire ceased to exist.

The Mughals were great builders; apart from the famous palaces, mausoleums, mosques and gardens which they built, a large number of public buildings of a more modest nature were needed for the government and the convenience of the public. They built or repaired several forts and fortresses, bridges, roads, canals, inns and houses. The department of construction was under the general supervision of the Mir Saman, because administratively it was one of the buyutat. However, sometimes a high official was asked to supervise the progress of some buildings. Alamgir I, when as a prince he was not posted away, from the capital, was

162. Abdul Hamid, *Qawad-i-Sultanate-i-Shah Jahn,* pp. 47-48.

163. Once a noble wore a dress so low that the skirts hid the feet. Alamgir I ordered that the skirts should be trimmed in the court. See *Ruqqaut-i-Alamgiri*, p. 46.

164. The Mughals never addressed the rulers as Sultans. They were often rebuked for exceeding the limits of tributaries.

assigned the duty.[165] The emperors took a personal interest in the construction of the more important buildings; the architects showed their plans to the emperor who gave the final approval.[166] Most of the important buildings bear the unmistakable impress of the personality of the monarch under whom they were built. The works department maintained an army of architects, engineers, craftsmen, carpenters and workers in stone.[167]

The Mughals did not have a seafaring navy worth the name; they never seem to have attached importance to the development of sea power, though they were seeing with their own eyes the consequences of neglecting it. However, this does not mean that they did not have a department. The head was called mir-i-bahr. He had the double duty of maintaining a fleet for fighting purposes and for policing the main inland waterways. The Mughals had a few vessels which could have made voyages in the open sea, but they were generally used in the broader rivers or their estuaries, the smaller craft was used on the other rivers. The care and the regulation of the seaports, as well as riverports, was in mir-i-bahr's charge. The levy of tolls from the merchants using the rivers and the ports for the conveyance of their merchandise also came under his jurisdiction.[168]

The classical Muslim writers divided the servants of the state into three main categories: the fighters were ashab-us-Saif or the masters of the sword; the accountants, clerks and other workers in the offices were ashab-ul-qalam or the masters of the pen; theologians and jurists were ashab-ul-amamah or men of the turban. The last class was not exactly the servant of the state, though some of them served it in certain important capacities. The first two categories were in every sense members of the public services; they were organized by Akbar into a single service in which they had a defined place, a mansab or a status.

165. *Dastur-ul-Amal-i-Agahi,* p. 33.
166. *Ain-i-Akbari,* p. 85.
167. *Ibid.,* p. 87.
168. *Ibid.,* pp. 234-36.

The word 'mansab' in the technical sense of a rank had been used prior to Akbar's reign; it was in use in Central Asia, but it did not imply any elaborate organization like the mansabdari system.[169] The idea of paying some civilian officers by putting them on the military payroll was also not unknown. The broad outlines of the system have been given by Abul Fazl in the Ain.[170] We are told that Akbar established sixty-six grades of mansabdars, ranging from the commanders of ten horsemen to those of ten thousand. The commands above five thousand were, however, limited in the first instance to the princes of royal blood. An examination of the list of mansabdars given by Abul Fazl reveals the existence of only thirty-three ranks in reality, the other thirty-three being only theoretical.[171] Not all the mansabdars were military officers. Those who held high civil posts were also mansabdars and were graded accordingly. The amalgamation of the civilian and military personnel into a single cadre has led some writers to believe that the Mughal government was a military government. The Mughal government can be defined only as a bureaucracy. There are instances of some civilians trying their talent in military exploits sometimes with disastrous consequences and sometimes with conspicuous success, but the instances of warriors and generals as civilian bureaucrats are very few in Mughal annals. The Mughals were wise in choosing their civilian officers so that their technical skills could be utilized to the greatest advantage.

The mansabdari system had many weaknesses, which contributed to the downfall of the Mughal empire. It was inefficient as a military machine. The Mughals depended upon the mansabdari system for the bulk of their armies. The inevitable result of the mansabdari system could have been either the militarization of the entire administration or the consequential abuses of military rule. The Mughal military machine, so efficient in the beginning, became more and more

169. Haider Dughlat, *op. cit.,* p. 103.
170. Abul Fazl, *Ain-i-Akbari,* p. 40.
171. Blochmann, *op. cit.,* p. 238.

clumsy and useless as time went on Akbar not only amalgamated the services but he also seems to have thought that anybody could be a military commander. His friend Birbal lost his life. On the northwest frontier because he obstinately refused to heed the advice of men who understood military matters; men like Todar Mal and Abdul Fazl were asked to fight battles and lead military expeditions.[172] The Mughals succeeded fairly well where they found that overwhelming numbers and resources could crush the enemy, but when they came across wily foes like the Marathas or guerrillas like the Pathan tribesmen. They found it difficult to deal with them.

The mansabdari system had its strong points as well. The most important factor was that it was based upon a recognition of merit and encouraged ability. It has been mentioned that no office was hereditary, everyone had to begin at the lower rungs of the ladder and could rise to the highest if he possessed the ability. The only exception was the appointment of the tributary chiefs like the Rajput princes. Even their talent and loyalty received adequate reward and mere chieftainship did not take the incumbent to the highest grades. The monarchs were fairly impartial in their encouragement of ability, they needed good servants and they encouraged them. The mansabdari system prevented the development of a feudal caste, however, it was not necessary to create this organization for this purpose. It weakened the tribal oligarchies which in the past had tended to grab power in times of stress. Its main advantage was that in spite of its weaknesses it strengthened the monarchy, because every mansabdar could look only to the monarch for promotion and advancement. Whatever its faults, the mansabdari system did enable the Mughals to give a good government to the people.

The Mughal military machine was not efficient. They succeeded in building up the empire because they were pitted against foes

172. Abul Fazl, *Ain-i-Akbari*, pp. 344-45.

who were even weaker and who could not match their resources to those of the Mughals. The repeated failure of the Mughals to hold Qandahar against the Persians was a sad commentary upon their military efficiency. They were equally unsuccessful against the Uzbeks. They changed too slowly; their methods had become inelastic. Even when faced with foes like the tribesmen in the north-west frontier or the Marathas, the Mughals failed to adapt their methods to the new situations, it took all the energy of a man of an iron will and unparalleled determination like Alamgir I to reduce the tribesmen and bring the Marathas to bay.

The Mughals developed sound traditions of financial administration. Their sources of income were well defined and so were the channels of expenditure. The system was built up by able administrators, some, but not all, of whom were of foreign origin. They had inherited well-tried traditions and principles which were based upon Islamic legal theory worked out in conjunction with local ideas and customs. Sher Shah had revived some institutions and reformed others and left an efficient financial administration. The anarchy following the collapse of the Sur dynasty had not completely wiped off these traditions, yet there had grown up abuses which Akbar undertook to remove with vigour. He also improved upon the previous institutions and developed them to a higher level of efficiency.

The jurists of Islam have divided the legal sources of the income of the state into two broad categories. The first of these consists of those dues which a Muslim pays as his religious obligation and which the state collects to expend in an organised and orderly manner; the second category includes the legitimate taxes which the state is entitled to collect for administrating the affairs of the inhabitants of the area under its control. The former classification applies to usher and zakat; the latter includes jiziyah, kharaj and such other taxes as the state can legitimately raise.

The zakat is prescribed by the Quran upon all Muslims who have a modest minimum of wealth which is technically called the nisab. The believer is required to pay the fortieth portion of it for charitable purposes. The Mughals did not collect this kind of zakat. The jiziyah has been mentioned in the Quran in the general sense of a tax; the word has an ancient origin in the Aramaic form of gezit. It came to be used early in the history of Islam in the sense of a poll tax levied upon the non-Muslim residents of a Muslim state. Its main purpose, in the beginning, was to meet the expenditure of administering the conquered territories when the non-Muslims were dominant in numbers. The payment of jiziyah was looked upon as a symbol of submission to the political power of Islam. It was from the basic concept of submission to the political jurisdiction of Islam that some extremists among the jurists drew their exaggerated notions regarding jiziyah being an instrument of humiliation for the jimmis.[173] It is also wrong to argue that jiziyah was the price which every non-Muslim was required to pay for being permitted to live in a Muslim state; this was neither the theory nor the fact. The jiziyah had a chequered history under the Mughals. Akbar abolished it. The argument seems to have been that all the citizens of the empire, irrespective of their faith, were liable to serve it, hence it would be unjust to levy jiziyah. The abolition continued to remain effective during the next two reigns. Shaikh Ahmad of Sarhind looked upon jiziyah as an institution of Islam and agitated for its reimposition. The reimposition, however, did not come until the reign of Alamgir I. As he himself was so strongly orthodox, he reimposed the tax.[174] Shah Jahan was also orthodox, but he had seen fit not to reimpose it, it is conceivable that ... he did not consider it legally necessary and was conscious of the political difficulties involved. The jiziyah was again abolished by Bahadur Shah I. Thus the tax was levied only for a part of the time during which the dynasty was strong

173. Barni, *Tarikh-i-Firuzshahi,* p. 290.

174. Ali Muhammad Kha, *op. cit.,* p. 296.

Alamgir did not look upon it as a source of income, because as such it was insignificant. To him, its imposition was a political measure, a matter of principle, the symbol of the prevalence of the law of Islam in his domains.

The Mughals seem to have levied the legal tax of a fifth upon minerals and certain categories of treasure troves. All unstamped bullion or coins, bearing the imprint of monarchs who ruled before the Muslim conquest buried in the earth and discovered now, had to pay a twenty per cent share to the state; the rest belonged to the owner of the land. The finder, if he was not the owner of the land, had no share.[175]

The Mughals do not seem to have enforced the Islamic tradition of sharing the war booty with the soldiers. The jurists prescribe a fifth of the booty as the share of the state and the rest goes to the soldiers. This was based on precedents when the soldiers were unpaid volunteers and did not receive regular salaries from the exchequer. The property of persons dying heirless and intestate was taken over by the state and earmarked for charitable and benevolent purposes.[176]

The legitimate revenue derived from the recognized demand of the state on agricultural produce was called mal (revenue). The taxes raised from manufacturers and merchandise were jihat if they were of financial importance; minor imposts raised by the central government and all imposts raised by the local authority were called sair jihat.[177] The distinction between the jihat and the sair jihat was never clear. They also used the term abwab for all additional burdens upon the people. The most burdensome of these cesses or abwabs was the rahdari, a toll levied upon the transport of goods from one place to another. The assignee or the chief through whose jurisdiction the merchandise passed supplied an escort to defend the merchant

175. Qureshi, *op. cit.,* p. 148.
176. Ali Muhammad Khan, *Jahangir,* p. 268.
177. Abul Fazl, *Ain-i-Akbari,* p. 12.

from highwaymen and charged a fee for the escort.[178] Another tax was the fee charged when the stolen property was restored by the authorities to the rightful owners having been recovered from the thieves. If the property could not be recovered the owner had to be compensated by those in whose jurisdiction the theft or the robbery had taken place. A fee as high as a quarter of the debt was charged to those who were helped in recovering debts. A considerable source of income was through the presents which were made to the emperor on various occasions.

The total revenue of the empire was estimated to be 5,131,353,000 dams under Akbar, 8,800,000,000 dams under Shah Jahan, and 13,599,963,822 dams under Alamgir I. There were 40 dams to a rupee.[179]

The Mughals adopted various methods of payment. A fair number of disbursements were made in cash. A proper pay order was made out and the treasurer concerned made the payment on obtaining a receipt. The other method was of paying salaries through the assignment of the revenue of a particular area: Those who received their salaries in cash were better off because they were saved all the bother of administering an area, which was not a part of their normal duties. The Mughals also made grants for benevolent purposes to the learned and the pious. The grants were made either in cash or in the form of assignments: These assignments were given in the form of revenue-free land. The assignment was known as Sayurghal or madad-i-maash. The cash allowances given for similar purposes were called surinah or wazifah, respectively depending on whether they were calculated on a daily basis or were awarded for longer periods.[180] A few assignments were given in perpetuity by Jahangir to some officers. These were called al-tamgha assignments. This was a freak revival of an old Timurid tradition. These grants were so-called because they were made out under the al-tangha

178. Khafi Khan, *Khaifiyat-i-Subajat-i-mumalik-i-mahrusah-i-Hindustan,* p. 220.

179. Najaf Ali, *op. cit.,* p. 21.

180. Abul Fazl, *Ain-i-Akbari,* p. 19.

seal. Al-tamgha assignments were also made for pious purposes.[181] Another method of payment that the Mughals adopted from the traditions of the land was to pay commissions on revenue for certain duties performed. Of the same nature were the perquisites paid to the village headman for assisting in the collection of the revenue and for helping in the maintenance of peace.

The Mughals built up large reserves. Their expenditure, except in times of stress, was always kept lower than their income. We are told that great wealth fell into the hands of Nadir Shah. The Mughal system of financial administration was complicated, but it served its purpose of preventing the defalcation of public funds. The principles of accounting and auditing were well understood. The ladies and the princes of the imperial family had their fixed salaries, beyond that they could not draw any money without imperial sanction, which was not always forthcoming even in the case of favourites.[182] The emperor himself had definite sums appropriated for his needs and seldom exceeded such appropriations. The stronger Mughal emperors were men who fully understood the principles of sound administration and knew how to control expenditure both at the government level and in the personal sphere. The Mughals did not so long as power was in their hands, indulge in such personal excesses; but they did maintain standards of splendour which have few parallels in history. Apart from other factors, the magnificence of the Mughal court created the halo around the monarch which made the dynasty stable and raised its prestige so high that it became a legend among the people in spite of its inherent military weakness.

The best-organised branch of the Mughal government was its agrarian administration. The Mughals devoted so much attention to agrarian matters because the state demand for agricultural produce was the mainstay of Mughal finance. Sher Shah devoted

181. Khwajah Yasin, *op. cit.,* p. 49.

182. Dara Shikoh's demand was refused by Sad-ullah Khan, who was supported by Shah Jahan.

considerable attention to it after the breakdown following the anarchy preceding his reign; therefore Akbar did not have to search very far for previous traditions. He, however, increased its efficiency and introduced some far-reaching reforms. The basis of the Mughal agrarian system was the recognition of the fact that the prosperity of the empire depended upon the well-being of the peasant Throughout the historical literature of the period, this sentiment is ubiquitous. He was to be protected, encouraged and helped.[183] The level of agricultural production was to be not only maintained but also continuously increased.

The peasant was the owner of his holding. All contemporary literature bears this out; the Ain, the law books and the dastur-ul-amals are all unanimous on the point.[184] This does not mean that there was no landless labour; such labour was employed by the peasant during harvest time when extra hands were needed, it was also employed upon lands held as suyurghals by scholars and divines who themselves could not work upon their holdings. If some of these were settled permanently as tenants, called mazari, they became hereditary and were entitled to sell or transfer their rights. Serfdom in any form was unknown, the peasant, as well as the landless labourer, was free to go anywhere he liked. The peasant was independent and even pugnacious and had to be treated with respect and consideration.

The traditions of self-governing village communities date back to prehistone times, the Mughals, like their Muslim predecessors, respected them and made them a part of their administrative system. It was with the cooperation of these communities that the agrarian administration could function; without the village accountant and qanungu, the machinery could not work. Similarly, the movement depended upon the peasant communities for the maintenance of law and order in the countryside. The brilliance and the opulence

---

183. Alamgir I's farman to Muhammad Hashim, Oriental Miscellany, 1798, pp. 51-52.

184. Qureshi, *op. cit.,* p. 176.

of the Mughal empire which so struck the Western travellers were based upon the well-being and prosperity of the peasant. The agrarian administration of the Mughal empire played no mean a part in keeping the peasant contented and happy.

The basic purpose of the organization of the community of Islam has always been the facilitation of the pursuit of virtue. The determination of the rights of individuals and groups is a necessary corollary of such a purpose because virtue implies the fulfilment of social and civil obligations. The Mughal Empire did not deviate from these traditions. In view of the basic philosophy of social and political organization in Islam, the Mughal emperors had a network of justice. The principles of the Shar were applied, in so far as it was feasible without injustice, to disputes arising between Muslims and non-Muslims. The Hindus had their own personal law and the provisions of the Shar regarding marriage, divorce and inheritance did not apply to them. A large number of cases were never referred to the courts instituted by the government. The villages, in accordance with hoary traditions of self-government, had panchayats, or council of the elders, who decided most disputes.

The muhtasib was theoretically responsible for the maintenance of the Islamic code of morals and behaviour.[185] It was his duty to ensure the smooth working of the Muslim society and to remove causes of public inconvenience and infringement of undisputed rights. His jurisdiction extended only to disputes relating to weights and measures, adulteration or fraud in merchandise and loans that were not disputed and yet which were not paid despite the debtor's capacity to meet his obligation. He was expected to perform a number of humanitarian duties. He was not to permit the maltreatment of slaves and servants.[186] He was to prevent cruelty to animals, so that they were not overloaded, made to work beyond their capacity or otherwise ill-used.[187] He was to arrange

185. Mawardi, p. 228.
186. *Ibid.*, p. 234.
187. *Ibid.*

for the care of foundlings and orphans.[188] School masters were not to be immoderate in inflicting punishment upon children.[189] He was responsible for the proper maintenance of the public utilities. He was to see that the water supply, the city walls, the public thoroughfares, the markets, hospices and inns were all maintained properly. The amenities existing for travellers were in his care. He was to see that river and seaports were kept in good condition and the boats were seaworthy and not overloaded.[190] In the city itself, it was his duty to prevent encroachments on public thoroughfares and squares, and to order the demolition of structures which were likely to collapse and endanger life.[191] The muhtasib has sometimes been called the censor of public morals. He was also expected to see that the public prayers were organized.[192] As a corollary, it was his duty to maintain the mosques in a proper state of repairs. The most important section of the muhtasib's duties was the supervision of the markets. He is reported to have said, 'Those guilty of adulteration do not belong to us".[193]

It is, however, quite possible that Akbar did not appoint muhtasibs because of his aversion to orthodoxy. The Ain assigns to the Kotwal some of the functions of the muhtasib. Alamgir I, however, thought it necessary to appoint a learned and pious theologian as the chief muhtasib of the empire to ensure the observance of the moral code of Islam. The person selected was Mulla Wajih of Turan with a salary of fifteen thousand rupees per annum.[194]

Grants were not made exclusively to Muslim institutions and scholars. A large number of Hindu temples, priests and scholars were recipients of such grants. Alamgir I is generally accused

---

188. Von Kraemer, *op. cit.*, pp. 292-96.
189. Mawardi, *op. cit.*, pp. 233-34.
190. Ibn Khaldun, *op. cit.*, p. 406.
191. *Ibid.*, p. 406.
192. Mawardi, *op. cit.*, p. 228.
193. *Ibid.*, p. 240.
194. Qureshi, *op. cit.*, p. 204.

by non-Muslim authors of discriminating against non-Muslims and persecuting them. The large number of documents found all over the subcontinent recording grants of land and money to Hindu temples, priests and others, belies the accusation.[195] The schools teaching Sanskrit and Hindu religion thus benefited. Abu-Fazl gives a list of the leading spiritual leaders and scholars who received grants from the Department of Religious Affairs. The first includes those whom Abul Fazl considers to be well versed in matters spiritual as well as intellectual. It includes twenty-one persons of whom mine are Hindus. Among those who were considered eminent in the field of spiritual attainments, he mentions fifteen, of whom four are Hindus. Among intellectuals who were learned both in religious and profane sciences, he mentions twelve, of whom none is a Hindu. Among those who were eminent philosophers he mentions twenty-two, of whom fifteen are Hindus, of physicians twenty-nine find mention of whom four are Hindus, of those who knew the religious sciences, he mentions forty-three of whom two are Hindus.

The Mughal empire has rightly been called a 'culture state'. Its patronage of learning and education drew scholars from the neighbouring Muslim countries. The patronage was not limited to religious education. Abu-Fazl mentions the subjects that were taught during Akbar's reign. They include ethics, arithmetic, accounting, agriculture, mensuration, engineering, astronomy, domestic science, civics and politics, medicine, logic, higher mathematics, history, the physical and mechanical sciences and theology.[196] It is true that in the sixteenth century the sciences had not made the rapid strides of the subsequent centuries, but the education imparted was liberal and comprehensive. Religion provided a strong base for this education. The secular sciences and rational disciplines received considerable impetus in the reign of Akbar by the arrival of Mir

195. Series of articles by Jnan Chand in Journal of Pakistan Historical Society, January 1958, April 1958, July 1958, October 1958, etc.

196. Abul Fazl, *Ain-i-Akbari,* p. 25.

Fath-ullah Shirazi who introduced the study of the works of the later Muslim philosophers like Muhaqqiq, Dawwani, Mir Sadr-ud-din, Mir Ghiyath-ud-din Mansur and Mirza Jan Mir. These works were introduced in the syllabus giving a great impetus to the study of philosophy.[197] Education made rapid strides under the continued patronage of the state. Alamgir I in particular made such liberal grants for educational purposes that even the smaller townships began to produce scholars of great eminence.[198] Apart from the patronage extended to formal education, the Mughal emperor paid large sums of money to men who devoted themselves to literature or poetry. Among the poets who thrived during the heyday of Mughal rule, some achieved immortality and have been recognized as masters wherever Persian literature has been appreciated. Of these Fardi, Urfi, Naziri, Saib, and Bedil reserve special mention. Abul Fazl, Faiji, Badayuni and Niamat Khan Ali were the better-known prose writers. Alamgir I perhaps wrote the best prose of the age. Princess Zib-un-nisa distinguished herself as a poetess and Dara Shikoh as a writer on religious, mystic and philosophical subjects. Akbar showed great interest in the translation of the Hindu classics into Persian. The Mahabharata, the Ramayan, the Singhasan Batisi, the Atharva Veda, the Harvansha and the Raj Tarangini were translated under his orders. Dara Shikoh is well known for his translation of the Upanishad which he called Sirr-i-Akbar. A translation of the Bhagavad Gita is also ascribed to him.

The Mughal empire has earned universal praise for its architectural achievements. Its buildings combine strength with refinement and delicacy. Akbar was a great builder and his department for the construction of buildings seems to have been well organized and extensive. Abul Fazl talks about the construction of fortresses, palaces, sarais, tanks, wells, schools and places of worship.[199] Akbar's greatest buildings were built at

197. Mir Azad Bilgrami, Maathir-ul-Kiran, p. 238.

198. Nadwi, Saiyyid Sulaiman, Hayat-I-Shibli, p. 1, gives details about the progress made in the eastern districts of modern Uttar Pradesh.

199. Abul Fazl, *op. cit.,* p. 85.

Fathepur Sikri, his capital near Agra, which was abandoned after having been occupied for fifteen years only. With Akbar's death, the style of architecture took a turn. The Islamic elements began to dominate and arches, domes and vaulted roofs came into greater use than pillars, beams and brackets became more calligraphic with the flowing lines of minarets and domes. Jahangir was not a great builder, but under Shah Jahan Mughal architecture reached the apogee of its development. Under Alamgir I the Deccan wars did not permit any extensive building programme. Besides, it was difficult to excel the Taj Mahal and the Jama Masjid. Yet the Padshahi mosque of Lahore and the Moti Masjid of Delhi are not insignificant contributions to architecture.

The Mughal emperors are also well known for their patronage of miniature paintings. Humayun found time in the midst of his exile to visit Tabriz to meet some of the renowned Calligraphists and painters there. He extended an invitation to Mir Sayyid Ali of Tabriz and Khwajah Abd-us-Samad who paid his respects to Humayun at Tabriz. They later came and joined Humayun. Akbar organized a regular department where under the guidance of these two masters others were trained and experiments were made in the use of new materials. A good number of Hindu artists also received training in the new technique. The school reached its zenith under Jahangir who was not only a great patron but also a connoisseur. The school maintained its excellence under Shah Jahan. The allied act of Calligraphy also received liberal patronage.

Music had reached its high-level mark under the Surs. Sultan Adil Shah was himself a great musician; he had two eminent pupils, Baz Bahadur, the ruler of Malwa and Miyan Tan Sen. About the latter Abul Fazl says, "A singer like him has not been in India for the last thousand years".[200] Tan Sen's grave at Gwalior is visited even today by the musicians of the subcontinent, who mention his name with great respect. The musicians were divided

200. Abul Fazl, *op. cit.*, p. 30.

into seven groups, one for each day of the week so that they might hold themselves in readiness if summoned for a performance.[201] The best composer and writer of songs, however, was Jagannath, who was on this account, given the title of Kaviraj. Alamgir I only tolerated music on occasions when traditionally it had become a part of the court ceremonial, especially on the occasion of certain celebrations.[202] On such occasions, the musicians were rewarded in the usual manner. But it seems that gradually he gave up the patronage of the art.

The nobles followed the example of their sovereign and every officer of high rank was a patron of learning and crafts. A good portion of the salaries paid to these officers was spent on the patronage of learning and culture. With such patronage the general cultural level was high.

In the remarkable cultural achievements of the Mughal empire, the Hindus participated fully. The architectural styles developed at the capitals were adopted by Hindu potentates. The visitor to Amber finds himself in the midst of a complex of buildings which were no different in style or spirit from the palaces of Agra and Shahjahanabad. Hindu nobles began to imitate the Mughals even in the construction of tombs. Though there was no tradition of the burial of the dead among the caste Hindus, the nobles began to build memorials to the dead, called samadhis, which were borrowed freely from the tomb architecture of the Mughals. The Mughal style even penetrated some of the temples. Its influence was even more marked in Jain temples. Many of the miniature painters at the court were Hindus. A parallel school, called the Rajput style, was developed by the Hindus who applied the techniques of the Mughal school to Hindu themes. Religious and mythological lore provided a rich source of inspiration to these artists. In Hindi itself, there was a continuation of the renaissance

201. *Ibid.*
202. Kazim, *op. cit.*, p. 107.

begun by the great Bhakti poets. In this period one of the greatest Hindi poets was Abd-ur-Rahim Khan Khanan, whose writings are part of the classics of Hindi. In the reign of Akbar and Jahangir lived the immortal Hindi poet, Tulsi Dasa who was one of the greatest poets of any time or any language. His Ramayan became almost the Bible of the Hindus. Undoubtedly the Mughal empire is a mirror of a composite culture where there was too much give and take between the Hindus and the Muslims.

CHAPTER-V

CONCLUSION

The sources of the study of the Mughal administration are scattered in many places. The Ain-i-Akbari of Abul Fazl is a mine of information but it does not give us much help in drawing a correct and detailed picture of the administrative machinery. Some information is given by the Dastur-ul-Anals or official handbooks which were prepared during the time of Shah Jahan and Aurangzeb. The so-called Manual of the Duties of Officers also gives useful information. The Iqbal-Namah Jahangiri by Mutamad Khan, the Padshah Namah of Abdul Hamid Lahori, the Tazuk-i-Jahangiri, the Tabaqat-i-Akbari of Nizam-ud-Din and Muntakhab-ut-Tawarikh of Badauni also give useful information. The writings of foreigners like Sir Thomas Roe, Bernier, Hawkins, Manucci, Terry, etc., also throw welcome light on certain aspects of the Mughal administration. The contemporary factory records of the English Company are useful in many ways.

The Mughal emperor was the head of the administration. According to the Quranic theory, the Mughal emperor was the ruler of the Muslims only, Amir-ul-Munnin, or commander of the true believers. He was nominally responsible to the Muslim public or Jamait for his conduct as a king. There was no check on his powers, but in actual practice, his autocracy was tempered by the fear of a rebellion. Customary law of the country also put a check. The Ulema had the power to depose a king but their Fatwas were a mere scrap of paper so long as the Mughal emperor had a strong army at his disposal.

Both Babur and Humayun acted upon the Islamic theory of kingship, but Akbar rejected the same. Instead of being the commander of the true believers only, he decided to become the king of all his subjects. His view was that in spite of thousand virtues, a king "cannot be fit for this lofty office, if he does not inaugurate universal peace, and if he does not regard all classes of men and all sets of religions with a single eye for favour." Akbar also believed that the king was superior to all human beings and was the shadow and vicar of God. In the words of Abul Fazl "Royalty is a light emanating from God, a ray from the sun, the illuminator of the universe, and argument of the book of perfection, the receptacle of all virtue." Akbar also believed that there should be a union of religious and secular leadership and that is why he tried to combine the two in his own person. Jahangir followed to some extent the ideal of his father. However, Shah Jahan and Aurangzeb again adopted the Islamic theory of sovereignty.

It is to be noted that the Mughal emperors enjoyed many prerogatives. There were some prerogatives which were the exclusive privilege of the sovereign and could in no case be exercised by any other person in the state. Jharokha-i-Darshan was one of those prerogatives. This custom was started by Akbar but was stopped by Aurangzeb. Every morning the emperor appeared on a balcony in the eastern walls of the Agra and Delhi forts when he was also there so that his subjects might have a full view of his face. Many people looked upon the sovereign as a partial incarnation of God and abstained from food and drink as long as they had not his Darshan. Another prerogative was chauki and Taslim-i-chauki. The principal nobles of the emperor had to mount guard and go around the palace by turns. They were required to offer obeisance in the direction of the palace at stated hours of the night. Another prerogative was known as Naqqara.

When the emperor held court or went out, a powerful kettledrum was beaten. This privilege could be exercised by other nobles with the permission of the king. The emperor alone had the prerogative to confer titles on his subordinates. Amirs and Mansabdars could only recommend suitable persons for this purpose, but the emperor alone could confer the titles. The emperor alone could affix his special seal. In special cases, he gave a vermilion print of his palm on farmans (edicts) issued by him. The emperor alone had the prerogative of ordering the mutilation of limbs. The witnessing of elephant fights was a special prerogative of the emperor. The emperor adopted the Hindu practice of Tula-dan or weighing against articles for charities. The emperor alone had the exclusive privilege of weighment against gold and jewels, while the others could get themselves weighed against other things.

The Mughal emperor in India did not recognise any khalifa as a superior overlord. At the time of the succession to the throne, the coronation ceremony was performed. It was not necessary that it must be performed at the capital of the empire. In the case of Akbar, it was performed in the Gurdaspur district of the Panjab. Murad and Shah Shuja proclaimed themselves as kings while away from the capital. When the new king sat on the throne, he was saluted by cries of 'Badshah Salamat'. Very often, the new king took up a new title Prince Saleem took up the title of Jahangir and Prince Khurram became Shah Jahan. Aurangzeb took up the title of Alamgir. The Khutba was read in the name of the king and coins were also struck in his name.

The Mughal emperors worked very hard. They kept longer hours and enjoyed lesser holidays. The king transacted his business in four different ways. He transacted state business in public while sitting in the Diwan-i-Khas-o-Am. In the Ghusikhana, the king held confidential consultations with his ministers and other officials as he cared to summon. The Ghuslkhana was a place of retirement for doing important work. Commanders of the expeditions were called to this place before they were sent to the front. Likewise, governors were summoned to this place before they were ordered to join their appointment. In the Ghuslkhana, Akbar had his religious discussions also and Jahangir had his cups of wine. Sometimes, the king summoned a few of his highest officials inside his private apartments to discuss and dispose of important business with them. Once a week, the king held the court of justice. This he did on Wednesdays when the Diwan-i-Am-o-Khas was converted into a court of justice. The aggrieved persons were presented before the Emperor by the superintendent of the court and the king tried to give justice to the people.

The orders of the monarch were issued usually through farmans. The procedure for drafting the farmans was very elaborate. Complete records were kept and special attention was paid to their authenticity. If a farman involved the grant of cash or jagir care was taken to see that it was passed on to the person for whom it was meant. There were five kinds of seals which were used for different purposes. One seal was used for titles, high appointments, jagirs and sanctions of large amounts. Another seal was used for letters to foreign kings. The third seal was used for judicial transactions. The fourth was used for all matters connected with the departments of the palace. The fifth seal was used for all other matters. The most important seal was the Uzuk seal and it was entrusted to the most dependable person. Some emperors used to keep the seal with their queens. In important farmans, the mark of the royal hand was put at the bottom.

The central administration of the Mughals was run by certain departments. Among them were the exchequer and revenue under the diwan-in-ala, the imperial household under the Khan-in-Saman or high steward, the military pay and accounts office under the imperial bakshi, canon law, both civil and criminal, under the chief qazi, religious endowments and charity under the chief sadar, censorship of public morals under the muhtasib, the artillery under the mir atish or darogha-i-topkhana, intelligence and posts under the darogha of dak chauki, mint under a darogha.

The office of the vakil seems to have come into prominence when Akbar was a minor and Bairam Khan acted on his behalf as deputy. After that, this office lost its importance. Although the title continued to exist, none was appointed to act for the emperor. It gradually lost its significance and completely faded away during the reign of Shah Jahan.

The Wazir was the prime minister. He was always the head of the revenue department, but that was in his capacity as diwan. On many ceremonial occasions, he acted as the representative of the king. All orders of payments had to be signed by him and all payments were made through his department only. Under the directions of the emperor, he himself passed orders. All questions concerning revenue affairs were settled by him and he consulted the emperor only in important cases. He had two assistants diwan of salaries and the diwan of crown lands. After the death of Aurangzeb, wazir became virtually the ruler of the state.

Bakshi was the paymaster. His influence extended to all departments of the central government. As all the officials, whether serving in the civil or military departments, were mansabdars and theoretically belonged to the military department, their pay bills were scrutinised and passed by the paymaster.

Khan-i-Saman was the lord high steward and was thus in charge of the emperor's department of manufactures, stores and supplies required for military and household purposes. He accompanied the emperor on his journeys and campaigns.

Sadar-us-sudur was the chief sadar of the empire. This office was filled by persons who had a very lofty character. He was the connecting link between the king and the people. He was the guardian of Islamic Law and the spokesman of the Ulema. It was his duty to look into and decide cases relating to grants. He distributed the money for charitable purposes.

Muhtasib was the censor of public morals. It was his duty to enforce the commands of the Prophet and suppress all those practices which were un-Islamic. Sometimes, they were asked to fix the prices of the goods and enforce the use of correct weights and measures. The muhtasib was required to go through streets with soldiers and demolish and plunder liquor shops, distilleries and gambling dens.

The chief qazi was the highest judicial officer and was responsible for the proper and efficient administration of justice. The qazis of the cities, districts and provinces were appointed by him. These qazis were helped by the muftis.

The diwan-i-buyutat registered the wealth and property of the deceased. He was required to calculate the amount due from the deceased to the state and deduct the same from his property. The balance was returned to the heirs of the deceased. His other duties were the fixation of the prices of the articles, making of provision for the royal karkhanas and the preparation of an estimate of their output and expenditure.

As artillery became an important branch of the army, the superintendent of artillery gained in importance. The mir atish was required to make arrangements for the defence of the imperial palace fort. He came into personal contact with the emperor and thus commanded great influence.

Darogha-i-dak chauki was the superintendent of intelligence and posts. He had his agents everywhere. Horses were stationed at various stages for the use of the messengers. The latter brought news from every part of the country. The superintendent was in charge of news writers and news-carriers.

Other important officials were the mir bahri (revenue secretary), mir barr (superintendent of forests), qur begi (lord standard bearer), akht begi (superintendent of the royal stud), mushrif (chief admiral and officer of harbours), nazir-i-buyutat (superintendent of imperial workshops), mustaufi (auditor-general), awarjah nawis (superintendent of daily expenditure at courts) khwan salar (superintendent of royal kitchen) and mir-arz (officer who presented petitions to the emperor).

The Mughal administrative system was in the nature of a military rule and was necessarily a centralized despotism. As far as the Muslims were concerned, the king was the head of the state and the church. As regards the non-Muslims, he was only their temporal head. The government did not interfere very much with the life of the people. Much of it was left undisturbed by the government.

The Mughal administrative system took its colour from the ways and creed of its sovereigns. They were foreigners who came from outside. They were accustomed to a certain system of administration and when they came to India, they transplanted the same in this country. The Mughal administration presented a combination of Indian and extra-Indian elements; or, more correctly, it was the Perso-Arabic system in the Indian setting. The principles of the government, their religious policies, their rules and taxation, their departmental arrangement and the very titles of the officials were imported readymade from outside India. But a compromise was effected with the older native system already in possession of the field and familiar to the people governed. The details of the imported system were modified for the local needs. The existing Indian practice and the customary law were respected as far as it did not run counter to the rout principles of all Islamic governments; and generally speaking in village administration and the lower rungs of the official ladder the Indian usage was allowed to prevail while the foreign swayed almost exclusively the court and the higher official circles.

The Mughal government was military in its origin and though in time it became rooted in the soil, it retained its military character to the last. All the civil servants were mansabdars or members of the army. Their names were arranged in the gradation list of the army as they were paid by the bakshi. Strictly speaking, there was no civil treasury at all. The land revenue system of the Mughals was based on the told Hindu system prevailing in the country.

The Mughal state was the largest manufacturer or the only manufacturer on a large scale. The state had to manufacture to satisfy its own needs which were very great. The emperor gave robes of honour or khilats to his mansabdars. Such a thing happened on many occasions.

The Mughal government was a highly centralized autocracy. The crown was the pivot of the entire administrative machinery. As the government was absolute and highly centralized, the written records multiplied. The Mughal government was called a paper government. A large number of books had to be maintained, e.g., copies of correspondence, nominal rolls, descriptive rolls, history of the services of the officers, news letters and dispatches, etc.

The attitude of the Mughal government towards law and justice was opposed to modern conceptions. It was the weakest in this matter. The government did not perform its responsibility of maintaining peace and security in the rural areas. The villagers were made responsible not only for the safety of their own property but also for the travellers on the neighbouring roads. The existence of the office of the faujdar is not denied, but the area within his jurisdiction was so large that it was out of the question for any individual to perform his duties satisfactorily.

The Mughal government was a despotism of a peculiar brand. Its absolute authority was never so interpreted by its rulers. The emperors left alone quite a large part of their subjects. They did not concern themselves with the religious beliefs of their people. Jahangir and Shah Jahan left even the religious practices of their subjects largely uncared for. When Aurangzeb stood forth as the champion of Sunni beliefs, he put down unorthodox practices without in any way trying to open windows into the souls of his subjects. Theoretically and to a large extent in practice, the judiciary was independent in a sense of its own in Mughal India. The administration of justice through Hindu pundits and qazis owed nothing to the king. The Mughal rulers made a few laws of their own but did not claim the right to do so. Aurangzeb had the Muslim law codified for the guidance of his qazis. Fatwa-i-Alamgiri is a digest of Muslim Law. The commentaries of Mitra Misra and Raghunandan on Hindu Law influenced its contemporary interpretation to a larger extent than the Fatwa-i-Alamgiri, Raghunandan and Mitra Misra did not write to the imperial orders and owed nothing to imperial favour.

The rulers were certainly Muslims, latitudinarian, indifferent or zealous. However, it cannot be said that their public administration was inspired by even the then-current ideas of Muslim polity. The organisation of the government, the ceremonies and the procedure in the Mughal court, and the method of raising revenue and recruiting public servants owed more to Indian traditions than to Islam. The vast majority of their subjects were non-Muslims and the Muslim rulers in India realized the impossibility of converting all of them to Islam. Hence, the Hindus were largely left in the enjoyment of their institutions.

BIBLIOGRAPHY

1. Abdul Aziz, *The Mansabdari System and the Mughal Army,* Lahore, 1942.
2. Abdul Hamid Lahuri, *Padshanama,* Calcutta, 1866.
3. Abd-us-Samad, *Insha-i-Abul Fazl,* Kanpur, 1872.
4. Abul Fazl, *Ain-i-Akbari,* Ed. Blochman, Calcutta, 1867; Akbarnamah, Calcutta, 1873.
5. Imam Abu Yusuf, *Kitab-ul-Kharaj,* Cairo, 1870.
6. Nicholas P. Aghnides, *Muhammadan Theories of Finance,* New York, 1916.
7. M.B. Ahmad, *The Administration of Justice in Medieval India,* Karachi, 1951.
8. Shaikh Ahmad Sarhindi, *Maktubat-i-Imam-i-Rabbani,* Lucknow, 1913.
9. C. Aitchinson, *A Collection of Treaties, Engagements and Sanads,* Calcutta, 1909.
10. Sir Thomas W. Arnold, *The Caliphate,* London, 1884.
11. Muhammad Tahir Ashna, *Shahjahanama.*
12. Mir Azad Bilgrami, *Maathir-ul-Kiram,* Lahore, 1913.
13. Zahir-ud-din Muhammad Babur, *Baburnamah,* London, 1921.
14. Abdul-Qadir, Badauni, *Muntakhab-ut-tawarikh,* Calcutta, 1864.
15. Muhammad Bakhtwar Khan, *Mirat-ul-alam,* Calcutta, 1957.

16. Bayazid Bayat, *Tadhkirah-i-Humayun wa Akbar*, Calcutta, 1941.
17. Francois Bernier, *Travels in the Mughal Empire*, London, 1916.
18. Rai Chandra Bhan Brahman, *Qawaid-i-Sultanate-i-Shah Jahan*, Calcutta, 1795.
19. Percy Brown, *Indian Painting under the Mughals*, Oxford, 1924.
20. Makhan Lal Roy Choudhury, *Din-i-Ilahi*, Calcutta, 1941.
21. *Dastur-ul-amal-i-Khalisah-i-Sharifah*, Edinburgh, 1930.
22. Elliot & Dowson, *History of India as told by its own Historians*, 8 volumes, London, 1867.
23. Sir Henry Elliot, *Bibliographical Index to Historians of Mohammadan India*, London, 1847.
24. W.A. Erskine, *A History of India under the First two Sovereigns of the House of Taimur*, London, 1854.
25. Muhammad bin Mansur Quraishi, *Adab ul-muluk wa Kifayat-ul-mamuluk*, Calcutta, 1917.
26. Muhsin Fani, *Dabistan-i-nadhahib*, Kanpur, 1904.
27. B.R. Grover, *Nature of Land Rights in Mughal India*, Delhi, 1961.
28. Gulbadan Begam, *Humayunamah*, London, 1902.
29. Irfan Habib, *The Agrarian System of Mughal India*, Bombay, 1963.
30. Hasan Ali Khan, *Tawarikh-i-dawlat-i-Sher-Shahi*, Delhi, 1950.
31. Bikramjit Hasrat, *Dara Shikuh, Life and Works*, Calcutta, 1953.
32. S.A.Q. Husaini, *Administration under the Mughals*, Dacca, 1952.
33. Ibn Hasan, *The Central Structure of the Mughal Empire*, London, 1936.
34. W. Irvine, *The Army of the Indian Mughals*, London, 1903.
35. W.H. Moreland, *India at the Death of Akbar*, London, 1020.
36. Peter Mundy, *Travels*, Vol. II, Travels in Asia, London, 1914.

37. Beni Prasad, *History of Jahangir,* Allahabad, 1940.

38. Ishwari Prasad, *Life and Times of Humayun,* Bombay, 1955.

39. Muhammad Sadiq Khan, *Shahjahanama,* Delhi, 1914.

40. Banarasi Prasad Saksena, *History of Shah Jahan,* Allahabad, 1932.

41. Jadunath Sarkar, *Mughal Administration,* Calcutta, 1952.

42. Sri Ram Sharma, *Mughal Government and Administration,* Bombay, 1951.

43. Vincent Smith, *Akbar, The Great Moghul,* Delhi, 1958.

44. Tara Chand, *The Influence of Islam on Indian Culture,* Allahabd, 1946.

45. Edward Thomas, *Revenue Resources of the Mughal Empire in India,* London, 1871.

46. R.P. Tripathi, *Some Aspects of Muslim Administration,* Allahabad, 1936.

47. Ahmad Yadgar, *Tarikh-i-Salatin-Afaghinah,* Calcutta, 1939.

48. Yusuf Husain Khan, *Selected Waqai of the Deccan,* Hyderabad, 1953.

49. Yusuf Mirak, *Mazhar-i-Shahjahan,* Karachi, 1961.

50. Jurji Zaydan, *Tarikhi-ut-tamaddum-ul-Islami,* Cairo, 1902.

51. Periodicals

1. *Bengal: Past and Present*, Calcutta.
2. *Indian Culture*, Calcutta.
3. *Islamic Culture*, Hyderabad.
4. *Journal of Indian History*, Allahabad, Trivandrum.
5. *Journal of the Asiatic Society of Bengal*, Calcutta.
6. *Medieval India Quarterly*, Aligarh.
7. *Oriental Miscellany*, Calcutta.
8. *Proceedings of the Indian History Congress.*

www.ingramcontent.com/pod-product-compliance
Ingram Content Group UK Ltd.
Pitfield, Milton Keynes, MK11 3LW, UK
UKHW042015190726
13854UKWH00005B/2293

9 789395 242448